De Stijl 1917–1931

Piet Mondrian

Composition with Red, Yellow, Blue and
Black, 1921
Compositie met rood, geel, blauw en zwart
Oil on canvas, 59.5 x 59.5 cm
Gemeentemuseum, The Hague

Carsten-Peter Warncke

The Ideal as Art
De Stijl 1917-1931

Benedikt Taschen

**This book was printed on 100 % chlorine-free
bleached paper in accordance with the TCF standard.**

© 1994 Benedikt Taschen Verlag GmbH
Hohenzollernring 53, D-50672 Köln
© 1990 artists' heirs for the illustrations, except:
© 1990 VG Bild-Kunst, Bonn, for the works of Arp, Bayer, Braque, van
Doesburg, Domela, van der Leck, El Lissitzky, Mondrian, Oud, Rietveld,
Taeuber-Arp and Wesselmann
English translation: Hugh Beyer
Production editor: Brigitte Hilmer, Cologne
Cover: Angelika Muthesius, Köln
Layout: Eckhard Neumann, Frankfurt am Main

Printed in Germany
ISBN 3-8228-0547-5
GB

Contents:

1: **De Stijl** 6

2: **The Universal Language** 14

3: **Overcoming Form** 30

4: **The Ideal as Art** 58

5: **Ideals in Practice** 88

6: **" … Creative Internationalism … "** 152

Notes 198

Literature 203

Biographical Notes 206

Gerrit Rietveld

Rietveld Schröder House, 1924
Seen from the street
50, Prins Hendriklaan, Utrecht

1: De Stijl

*"The demand for pure means of expression,
first formulated by De Stijl,
has become a fact."*
Theo van Doesburg[1]

De Stijl is all around us: clothes, curtains, furniture, carpets and packaging – *De Stijl* has left its mark on all of these, so that the design principles developed by artists many decades ago are now applied in a large variety of different contexts.

De Stijl has made a noticeable contribution to our modern world. Many things which are familiar, normal and taken for granted go back to the ideas and inventions of modern artists. Their daring forms, which were often considered strange and shocking at the time, have been imitated, varied and developed a thousand times since then, so that they are now part of our normal visual experience. Towards the end of the 20th century, with its fast development, this creative period of fundamental innovation has long been concluded. The formal language of modern art has turned out to be suitable for the creative requirements of our industrial societies in the Age of the Machine.[2] This undisputed value turns the works of their founders into classics. Names of artists have become synonymous with modern art, and their popularity is the best indication of their historical and artistic significance, even though their influence is not always easy to discern.

Piet Mondrian, one of the very first *De Stijl* artists, is a good example. His art means far more than just the paintings of an individual: they mark an entire principle, clearly demonstrating a fundamental innovation in abstract, classical art. There is no depiction of objects, and his paintings are composed in an elementary way: planes in the three primary colours – red, blue and yellow – as well as black, white and grey, and simple rectangles, surrounded by black lines – that is all. Nevertheless, no two paintings are alike, thus showing that his art is simple, but not simplistic. But although his artistic means are simple, the actual works are not. A comparison of Mondrian's paintings with those of other *De Stijl* artists shows their wide range of expressiveness. While they were following the *De Stijl* movement, they all worked with elementary forms and colours, though their works displayed considerable differences.

De Stijl was the title of a Dutch fine arts magazine, published between 1917 and 1931.[3] Set up by a small group, it became a reservoir for kindred spirits, a forum for discussing new directions in modern art and the mouthpiece for its propagation. This is where artists who saw themselves as radically progressive published critiques, theories, manifestoes and new works. *De Stijl* was soon accepted as the name of their

Vilmos Huszár

De Stijl, front cover
The newspaper was published in this form from the first issue in October 1917 to the twelfth issue of its third year in November 1920

Piet Mondrian

Composition in Red, Yellow and Blue, 1921
Compositie met rood, geel en blauw
Oil on canvas, 80 x 50 cm
Gemeentemuseum, The Hague

Theo van Doesburg

Composition XIII, 1918
Compositie XIII
Oil on canvas, 29.5 x 29.5 cm
Stedelijk Museum, Amsterdam

creative work, going down in history as the "Dutch contribution to modern art".[4]

De Stijl is a variant of the kind of abstract art which emerged in Modernism and became characteristic of it. It was the explicit intention of the artists that this new form of art should not be representational, illustrative or narrative, as the older form of art had been which was considered to be conventional at the time. On the contrary: it was to bear no relation to the world of objects or the imitation of its shapes, but should be understood entirely in its own terms. *De Stijl* also distinguished itself from other varieties of abstract art in its use of geometrical figures in compositional constructions which almost seemed technical. This meant that Dutch *De Stijl* was very much part of a general European movement – so-called Constructivism. The formal rationalism of *De Stijl* was based on its comprehensive, programmatic claim that a new, ideal world should be created by means of the basic elements of fine art. Art was seen in *De Stijl* as avant-garde: it was able to show something as a concrete result which had not yet been attained in the development of society at large – a state of ideal harmony. This is also why *De Stijl* was not limited to any particular art form, but oriented towards comprehensive realizations from the very beginning.

Gerrit Rietveld

Red/Blue Chair, 1918–1923
Rood-blauwe leunstoel
Beechwood with red and blue varnish,
88 x 68 x 64 cm
Stedelijk Museum, Amsterdam

The universality of *De Stijl* is reflected in the list of artists who gathered around this movement at least part of the time. Apart from the painters Piet Mondrian, Bart Anthony van der Leck and Friedrich Vordemberge-Gildewart, it also included the painter and architect Theo van Doesburg, the furniture designer and architect Gerrit Rietveld, the painters and sculptors Georges Vantongerloo and César Domela, the architects and designers Jacobus Johannes Pieter Oud, Robert van 't Hoff, Jan Wils and Friedrich Kiesler, the painter and designer Vilmos Huszár, the poet Anthony Kok, the interior designer Truus Schröder-Schräder, the film producer Hans Richter and the designers Peter Röhl and Werner Graeff.

One of the artists who was particularly influential in *De Stijl* was Theo van Doesburg. Having taken the initiative to set up the magazine, he continued to work as its editor-in-chief right until the end. Most programmatic statements came from him. And if *De Stijl* had a certain charisma about it that made it famous far beyond the Dutch borders, it was due to van Doesburg's energy, untiring efforts and amazing resourcefulness. He was the driving force behind the movement and the central reference point for the various artists. Their collaboration took extremely different forms in the course of the years. After all, *De Stijl* was a forum and not a tight, homogeneous group. Apart from the smaller, Dutch circle, the magazine also published the works of Russian Constructivists like El Lissitzky, Italian Futurists like Gino Severini and Dadaists like Kurt Schwitters, Jean Arp and Sophie Taeuber-Arp. And although everybody had the same aim, their views differed as to how this aim might be achieved, so that there were disagreements and splits. Even while *De Stijl* was still being published, Mondrian had an argument with van Doesburg and left the group. Others had already done so before him, and Pieter Zwart, an architect and designer who was extremely important for the movement, never even joined their ranks. This was in fact quite typical of *De Stijl,* with its open-minded and rather undogmatic diversity combined with the discipline of binding, fundamental intentions. The artistic movement was therefore not just historically influential, it had a history of its own, and knowledge of this history explains the breadth of creative endeavours and diversity of what was achieved.

Indeed, these achievements were quite impressive. The most important 20th-century artists include not only Mondrian and van Doesburg. With his *Red/Blue Chair* and the *Rietveld Schröder House*, Gerrit Rietveld created two early and influential works – one in modern furniture design and the other in architecture. Their stylistic consistency and almost archetypal persuasiveness are still unparalleled. And J.J.P. Oud, one of the first men to promote International Style, was an outstanding architect who became famous and influential far beyond the Netherlands.[5]

With its universal intentions and the exemplary character of its works, *De Stijl* has become a source of inspiration for modern design, and its comprehensive significance is comparable only to projects such

Tom Wesselmann

Still Life No. 20, 1962
Collage and assemblage of paint, paper, wood,
light bulbs, switch, etc.
104.14 x 121.92 x 13.97 cm
Albright-Knox Art Gallery, Buffalo (N.Y.)
Courtesy Seymour H. Knox

as the *Bauhaus*. Any intensive discussion of the history of classical modernism, especially in the last few years, has emphasized the significance of *De Stijl* for our century. For a long time now *De Stijl* art has been an object of academic research, the works of deceased artists have found their way into public art galleries, and their analysis has yielded significant new insights into historical contexts and processes.[6]

De Stijl is an historical phenomenon, though one that continues to exist in everyday life. Oud's café in Rotterdam, *De Unie*, which was built in 1925 and destroyed during the Second World War, has been rebuilt (though not in an entirely authentic form and not in the same place). The *Rietveld Schröder House* in Utrecht was given its interior design when it was built and is now accessible to the public as a museum. And the little Frisian town of Drachten, where Theo van Doesburg designed a brightly coloured housing estate in the Twenties, has been given back its original exterior.

Where lack of understanding and overt rejection used to dominate, this has been superseded by admiration and pride. Mondrian's paintings have attained the status of icons of classical modernism, so that they themselves are now the objects of more recent art, e.g. Tom Wesselmann or Roy Lichtenstein.

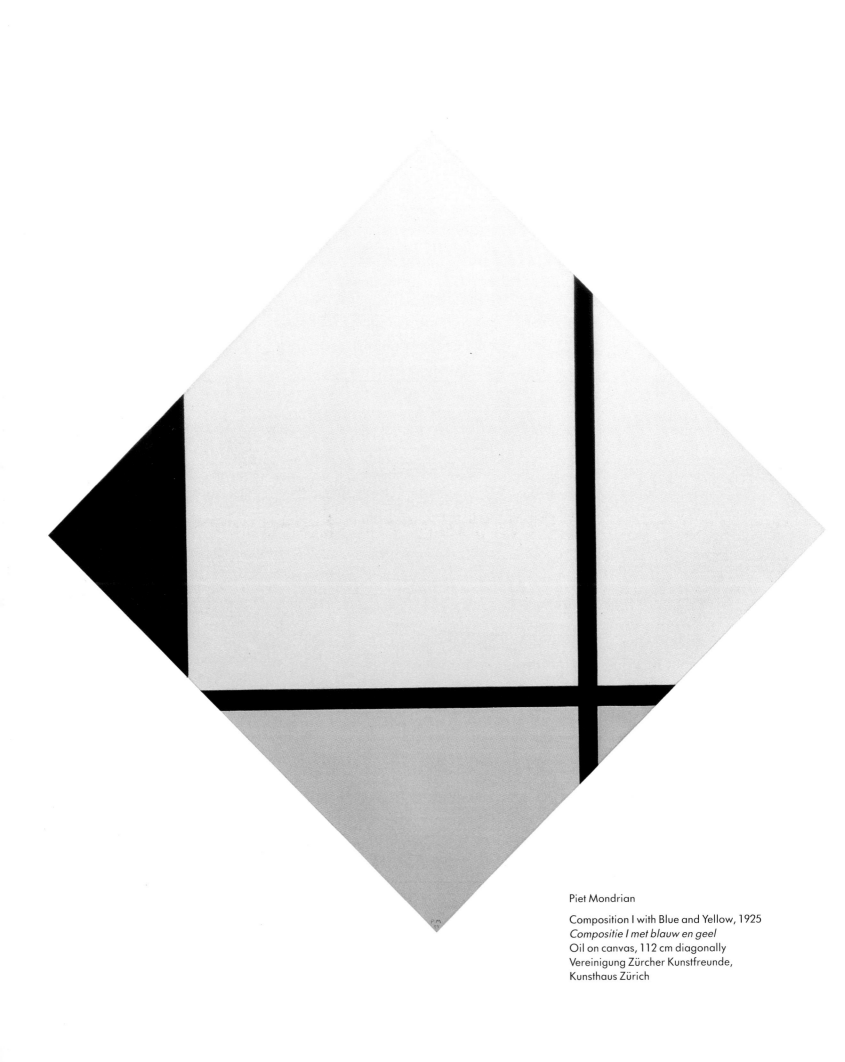

Piet Mondrian

Composition I with Blue and Yellow, 1925
Compositie I met blauw en geel
Oil on canvas, 112 cm diagonally
Vereinigung Zürcher Kunstfreunde,
Kunsthaus Zürich

2: The Universal Language

If *De Stijl* paintings are so elementary and seem so simple, why are they so fascinating? How could *De Stijl* become one of the foundations of modern art? The answer lies in the paintings themselves. And it is irrelevant whether they were created by the artists directly in conjunction with the debate in the magazine or only after the rupture between van Doesburg and the others. The important ideals of *De Stijl* were still very much alive at the time and their relevance can be assessed very clearly.

The paintings of Mondrian, Vantongerloo, van Doesburg and Huszár - all from the Twenties — are variations of the same idea. *De Stijl* was a conscious return to the basic principles of art itself: colours, shapes, planes and lines. The *De Stijl* artists did more with these elements than create their own imagery — though that in itself would have been an historic achievement. They developed a new metaphorical language, graphically displaying an ideal counter-world to reality. Mondrian's diamond-shaped *Composition I with Blue and Yellow* from 1925 (p. 14) is a typical solution to the problem. To start with, the lozenge attracts our attention as an unusual format. It is a square balanced on one corner. At first glance, it does not seem to offer anything very interesting: three black lines, two colourful and two colourless planes — and no more. But Mondrian, who enjoys juggling with the dialectic of visual concepts, somehow succeeds in holding us spellbound. Closed and open shapes as well as density, width, colour and plane are seen in a tense and therefore ingenious relationship with one another as they catch our attention. But what does this picture actually show? What can we understand without difficulty? Virtually nothing.

The apparent facts can easily be listed: blue in the left-hand corner, yellow on the right, white at the top and grey at the bottom. There is a thin black line on the right, a thick one on the left and a horizontal one between the top and the bottom. But the moment we use such words to describe the actual features of the painting, we have fallen prey to a rather arbitrary approach. Take for example the lines and their role within the overall composition. Lines between planes are borders. But here? It is true, of course, that the thick black line on the left separates the blue corner from the white plane next to it. But what about the line on the right where it runs straight through the white plane? Or does it separate two white planes from each other which differ in size? The oblique line at the bottom of the painting, on the other hand, separates the white from the grey planes. Yet it cannot be regarded as a border in the sense that it delineates a shape, because the white plane on the left remains open, so that everything only closes up outside the canvas. However, this is an intellectual construction which is suggested by the artist. It cannot be found in the painting itself. We must (and can) easily imagine the intersection of the thick and thin black lines somewhere outside the painting, though we cannot see it. This part of the painting

Piet Mondrian

Composition with Red, Yellow and Blue, 1921
Compositie met rood, geel en blauw
Oil on canvas, 39.5 x 35 cm
Gemeentemuseum, The Hague

Theo van Doesburg

Counter-Composition VIII, 1924
Contra-compositie VIII
Oil on canvas, 100 x 100 cm
The Art Institute of Chicago, Chicago
Courtesy Peggy Guggenheim, 1949.216

Piet Mondrian

Composition with Two Lines, 1931
Compositie met twee lijnen
Oil on canvas, 114 cm diagonally
Stedelijk Museum, Amsterdam

Georges Vantongerloo
Composition y = $\frac{2x^2}{5}$ with Red, 1931

Composition y = $\frac{2x^2}{5}$ avec rouge
Oil on canvas, 12.5 x 16.8 cm
Private collection

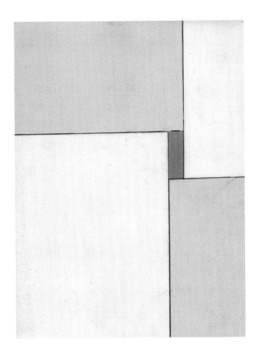

just does not exist — and yet somehow it does, due to the powerful suggestiveness of what we can see in the painting. Mondrian's painting transcends itself.

But not only at this point: because of its diamond shape, this is true for all sides. Since nothing in the painting has firm borders, we involuntarily continue the painting in our mind; we follow the lines and can easily imagine an enlargement of the coloured and colourless planes. In fact, it would seem to us as if we were actually extending the painting, because the lozenge is a square and therefore a perfect shape, whereas most sections in the painting are irregular.[7] Even these few compositional elements show the artist's amazing ingenuity and the powerful language of his elementary visual devices. It remains remarkable that Mondrian should have succeeded in combining the disparate parts of the painting in such a harmonious structure. Again, he could only have achieved this through the multifaceted ambiguity that pervades the various elements of the painting. Because of its dark shade, blue appears to be heavier than yellow and we therefore feel that it is behind the yellow. Front and back are represented by blue and yellow in the painting. Balance is achieved in the way in which they neutralize each other by virtue of the different-sized planes. Among the colourless planes this is matched by the relationship between grey and white.

To sum up, due to the accurate, detailed and carefully premeditated weighting, everything in this painting is questionable but at the same time balanced, so that the various elements add up to a complex and harmonious whole — a perfect harmony of opposites. It seems as though the painter were juggling with counterpoises, equivalences and seemingly established facts which he then questions. The artist has used his license to form a suggestive, immediately accessible and therefore, as it were, happy and perfectly balanced world. As blue is heavier and seems deeper than yellow, the blue plane can be larger than the yellow one which crowds into the foreground. But although the massive, opaque blue competes with the empty white, the picture does not disintegrate, because the two parameters of brightness and colour value are in many ways related to each other. As a result, yellow not only balances out blue, but also brings white to the fore, thus accentuating a colour that normally lacks substance. But for the dividing line in the white plane, we would not even notice the special significance of such zones. What is communicated to the viewer within a matter of seconds is a highly complex ensemble of different artistic parameters. These are of an elementary kind and therefore accessible to everyone. Like all *De Stijl* paintings, the picture transcends all language barriers.

Georges Vantongerloo's compositions are examples par excellence, even though they were painted after he had left *De Stijl* (pp. 20 and 79). Colours are surrounded by white and grey, a small plane is balanced against a large, white one, an upright plane against one on its side, and colourful against colourless. In their inextricable opposition to each other, they form a stable equilibrium. Any intrinsic optical value that the colourful planes might have is reduced again by their relatively

Theo van Doesburg

Composition XVIII, 1920
Compositie XVIII
Oil on canvas, 35 x 35 cm each
Rijksdienst Beeldende Kunst, The Hague

Theo van Doesburg

Composition XXII, 1920–1922
Compositie XXII
Gouache on paper, mounted on cardboard,
45.7 x 40.6 cm
Stedelijk Van Abbe Museum, Eindhoven

small size compared with other planes. Conversely, the colourless planes gain in importance by being much larger, so that they can defy the strength of the more vivid colours.

As if created specially to make a point, Theo van Doesburg's related compositions of 1920 demonstrate this vocabulary of form (p. 21). Light blue, red-orange, grey, black and white confront each other in different-sized planes and combine to form configurations that are also different each time. The effect of each plane is dependent on its position and size within the entire work. If a grey plane is large, then the white one has to be either small or narrow, an imposing blue has to be matched by an equally powerful orange, and grey and white also have to be related to each other in the same way. In principle the different parts are identical, though they vary in shape, so that their combination yields something new each time. Nothing is fixed in this system, except for the basic elements and the aim of balancing the different forces. This presupposes that all our seemingly secure assumptions should be questioned again and again. Traditional paintings would have started off with definitions, but these are now no longer accepted or applicable. The normative power of tacit agreements has been broken. The conventional relationship between lines and planes, shape and surface, depiction and picture plane are no longer valid.

Van Doesburg and Mondrian's classically reduced compositions of 1924 and 1931 (pp. 18 and 19) demonstrate artistic licence, destroy traditional conventions and display the vitality of a new attitude toward familiar things. The simple canvas ground is white, and the picture stands out against it. But are the black beams in van Doesburg's painting really the picture? Would it not be equally plausible to say that the white planes have been painted onto the black background? It is the logic of a *trompe d'oeil* painting, for depending on our point of view it does not allow any passive acceptance of facts. In this way the relationship between the elements causes extraordinary sensations!

The black beams are of the same thickness in van Doesburg's paintings, whereas Mondrian's lines are much thinner and differ in width, so that they create stability and tension at the same time. Width traditionally suggests heaviness and therefore tends to occur at the bottom – though not in van Doesburg's art. This is why there can be this reversal of background and picture. Nor do the black planes penetrate each other, though they do so in Mondrian's paintings, which seem like simple configurations of two crossed lines. However, they not only divide up a plane, they also delineate it, create new planes and define visual weights. Large planes are poised against small ones in fragile suspension. Any rigid symmetry that might create order has been subtly avoided, and not a single proportion corresponds to another. The edge and the centre complement each other as necessary opposites; they are either marked or deliberately avoided and are therefore just as effectively present as the depicted size. Mondrian's paintings of 1920 and 1921 have the same orderly scheme of components as their starting point (pp. 17 and 23), with a steady increase in the degree of reduction.

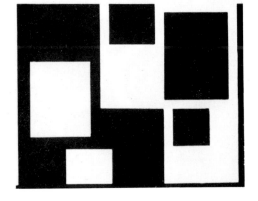

Vilmos Huszár

Composition VI, 1917
Compositie VI
Linocut, 11.4 x 14.2 cm
Stedelijk Museum, Amsterdam

Piet Mondrian

Composition with Red, Yellow and Blue, 1920
Compositie met rood, geel en blauw
Oil on canvas, 51.1 x 60 cm
Stedelijk Museum, Amsterdam

Piet Mondrian

Draughts Board composition, dark colours, 1919
Compositie dambord, donkere kleuren
Oil on canvas, 84 x 102 cm
Gemeentemuseum, The Hague

This is precisely how they demonstrate the persuasive power of principles. The reduction to a small number of things that are basically always the same does not necessarily mean poverty of expression – on the contrary. It is ingenuity at its best, and subtle nuances become tangible. In a world of images that have been reduced to the most basic concepts, any change, however small, in the structure of the components – and indeed any divergence of individual proportions – is a sensation; an exciting message. It is certainly true that we have to accept and enter into this system of shapes – a system which is so radical that it does not tolerate indifference – for the forcefulness of this elementary system does not permit us to avoid it. Any abstract relationships, such as large versus small, are shown as arbitrary definitions, and their interdependence becomes immediately comprehensible and can be perceived directly. We do not begin to analyse the subject until later, when we reflect upon what we have seen.[8]

Less is more – this is an old wisdom of art which *De Stijl* artists have put into practice with great consistency. Vantongerloo's studies, van Doesburg's compositions and Mondrian's paintings all use the same methods in a new way. The different effect of paintings that have their starting point in the middle or at the edge can be seen in a comparison of Mondrian's compositions of 1920 and 1921. Van Doesburg's painting (p. 21) from the same period mediates between the two extremes, though without being dull or insipid. Centre and periphery, surface and depth, and background and height are interlocked in an impenetrable and inseparable structure. The yellow plane, which is comparatively

24

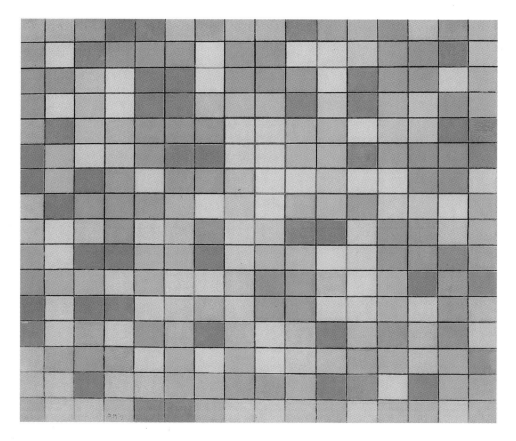

Piet Mondrian

Draughts Board composition, light colours, 1919
Compositie dambord, lichte kleuren
Oil on canvas, 86 x 106 cm
Gemeentemuseum, The Hague

large, has been pushed to the left of the middle axis. Near the edge, however, it is delineated by a white band, so that it also seems pushed from the edge towards the middle. Paradoxically, it seems suspended and at the same time firmly anchored, because the forward thrust of the bright yellow is intercepted by the aggressive signal of the red. In this way a balance is created between top and bottom which is similar to that between the edge and the middle. In such a picture the centre and the periphery mutually imply one another and are intricately linked as concrete, separate entities. In Mondrian's paintings, on the other hand, the relationship is the exact opposite, with a one-sided emphasis on the edges.[9]

In the positive/negative interplay of artistic design any definition automatically turns into its exact opposite. This is why some of Vantongerloo and Mondrian's paintings are similar and therefore variants of each other. Each group of works is characterized by abundance and reduction. Their construction principle can be understood as moving either from the centre or the periphery. The different artistic methods can be contrasted with each other and the rich abundance of possible changes in central distribution can be classified in this way, but it is impossible to find a basic difference. Regularity and the lack of it can only ever be effective in relation to the message of each picture. Mondrian's *Draughts Boards* (pp. 24 and 25) are based on distances that are the same everywhere: a plane is created which consists of squares the same size, just like on an ordinary draughts board. The distribution of the colours, however – asymmetrical, and with totally uneven clusters –

counterbalances this feature, so that it contributes to a synthesis of two disparate structures. The same can be found in some of Vantongerloo's paintings: although they do not have a whole scheme of squares that are strictly the same size, they do have some repetitions of this kind with an arbitrary distribution of colours.

Abundance, arbitrariness and irregularity are bound to cause a state of unrest. But the dynamic is toned down again by the static force of balance, and the contrasts, too, are absorbed in a synthesis, so that there is harmony. The various different schemes result in an emphasis on different focal points, so that each individual painting becomes a demonstration of a different approach. This is one way, it seems to be saying, but there are also others!

The result, which is always the same, can be achieved in an infinite number of ways. Each of them is equally concrete and has its own independent status. It is irrelevant in principle whether many or few of the elementary methods are used, although this is extremely important for each painting. The result may be basically the same, but it always looks different. Whether only black and white are used or – instead – the whole gamut of basic colours as well as the scale of colourless tones ranging from white through grey to black, it is a dialectical difference which occupies the negative and positive poles of abundance versus restriction and economy versus wealth, leaving open an immeasurable range of intermediate stages.

There can be no doubt that Mondrian, van Doesburg, Vantongerloo and Huszár, as well as Domela and Vordemberge-Gildewart (who did not join *De Stijl* until later), were all independent artistic personalities with different creative temperaments. Mondrian's construction of squares and lines is a process that leads to harmony and rest to the extent that we forget everything that might be reminiscent of processes, while van Doesburg's pictures show a completely different approach to dynamics, with colour squares that border on each other harshly and are right next to each other. This dynamic has the rank of an elementary force which can only be tamed with great difficulty and changed in such a way that the well-balanced painting oscillates in its visual impact, pradoxically demonstrating harmony as vibrating restfulness. However, such a contrast does not go beyond the confines of the system. Unadulterated, without any borrowings from the world outside themselves and therefore totally self-sufficient and purist in their consistency, these paintings speak for themselves. Variations to this language are possible and indeed permitted.

However, there is a critical limit: the similarity to imitations of shapes outside the painting, i.e. associations with actual shapes and the danger that works of art might serve as mere illustrations. Bart van der Leck's paintings (both on p. 29) demonstrate this point. Painted in 1918 and 1922, they show no more than planes of red and blue against a white background, together with yellow and black. The white is not limited anywhere but expands in all directions, so that its mass is far heavier than all the other planes. Because of their irregular shapes, they

Georges Vantongerloo

Study, 1919
Etude
Casein, 30 x 22.5; 28 x 30 cm
Private collection, Switzerland

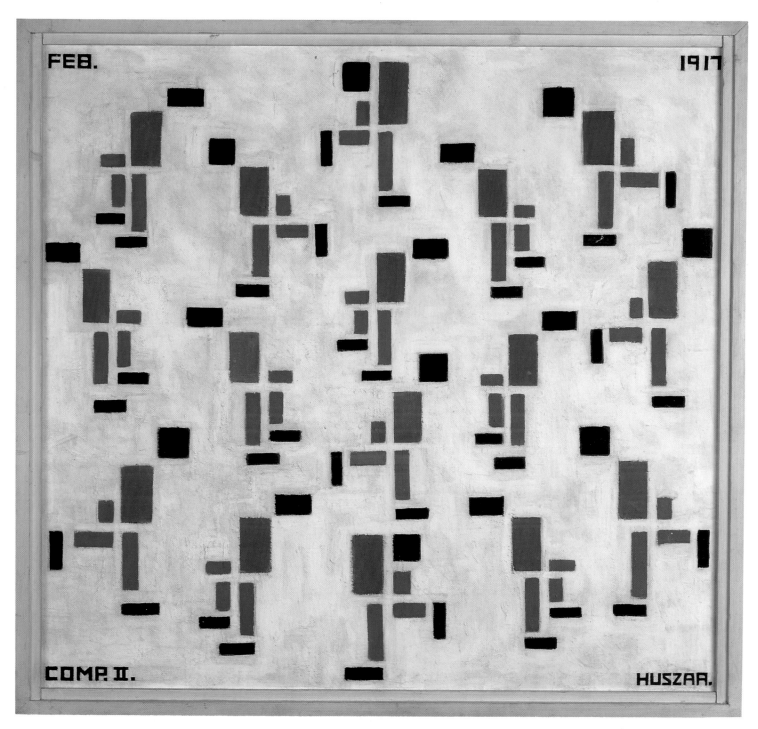

Vilmos Huszár

Composition II (The Ice-Skaters), 1917
Compositie II (De schaatsenrijders)
Oil on canvas, 74 x 81 cm
Gemeentemuseum, The Hague

Bart van der Leck

Composition 18-21, 1918–1920
Compositie 18-21
Oil on canvas, 101 x 100 cm

This painting was originally owned by Truus
Schröder-Schräder and hung in the Rietveld
Schröder House from 1925 until her death.

seem as if they had been imposed onto the white, even if the process was technically the reverse, i.e. the canvas was painted white and the other colour planes created in this way. As a result the system of colour shapes generates a deliberate association with the real world, and we can discern a horseman and a still life with a wine bottle. Whereas in the classic paintings of Mondrian, van Doesburg and Vantongerloo real-life associations cannot be ruled out completely (though they always seem like inappropriate additions), they are an important part of van der Leck's picture and also of his message.

Van der Leck's message is totally different. His paintings are not radically abstract, i.e. non-representational. They are abstractions or schematic representations of existing objects. Van der Leck shows us the general principles as reflected in specific instances. He reduces painting techniques to basics and turns them into compositions that remain linked to everyday experiences of the outside world, despite all stylization of reality.[10] The works of Mondrian, van Doesburg, Domela, Vantongerloo and Vordemberge-Gildewart speak an utterly different language – a language that was totally new at the time.

The effect was – and still is – stunning. Indeed it has not lost any of its inner logic over the years. A counter-world was created. *De Stijl* reconciles different principles without losing any of their specific effects. It is an imagery based on contrast, though in its compositions this imagery is given a synthesis or a unity on a higher level that neutralizes it again.

The aesthetic element in fine arts has always created a counter-world vis-à-vis reality and transformed its reflection into something beautiful. The consistent refusal to depict anything from the real world releases a pure aestheticism and changes it from mere pleasure into a potentially critical force that makes all other principles of artistic endeavour appear insipid. Different degrees of light, colourfulness, the signalling power of colours and the spaciousness of colourful planes, the weight of shapes and the concepts of borders and shapes – all these are now treated as questionable and as things that can be superseded. However, they are by no means rendered invalid. For it is not just the purely technical elements of art that remain concrete, but even the actual content, a content which is always associated with the elementary means, especially with primary colours, and is always implicitly present. In this sense *De Stijl* is part of an ancient tradition.

Even contemporary avant-garde artists took it for granted that colours were symbolical, e.g. blue was heavenly, intellectual and male, yellow was female, and red was powerful, etc.[11] However, these concepts are neutralized in the contrast between dimensions that have been reduced to their principles and united as opposites. In fact, the radical nature of this imagery goes so far as to transcend the very foundations of depiction as such. To what extent, for example, can these pictures be called "drawings"? The means of expression in this art are elements of a very basic kind, so that everyone can understand them. Despite its universality, it is a highly principled language, and the only thing that is left is its ideal perfection.[12]

Bart van der Leck

Still Life with Wine Bottle, 1922
Stilleven met wijnfles
Oil on canvas, 40 x 32 cm
Rijksmuseum Kröller-Müller, Otterlo

Bart van der Leck

Horseman, 1918
Ruiter
Oil on canvas, 94 x 40 cm
Rijksmuseum Kröller-Müller, Otterlo

Piet Mondrian

Church Tower at Domburg, 1910/11
Kerktoren te Domburg
Oil on canvas, 114 x 75 cm
Gemeentemuseum, The Hague

3: Overcoming Form

When the *De Stijl* magazine was first printed in October 1917, it probably seemed like the mouthpiece for a radically new form of art. The first issue, published under Theo van Doesburg as editor-in-chief, was helped financially by a full-page advertisement of a parquet-floor company called Bruynzeel and contained several programmatic articles by Piet Mondrian, Bart van der Leck, Jacobus Johannes Pieter Oud and Anthony Kok. The cover was given its unmistakable appearance by Vilmos Huszár. But the magazine was not really a mouthpiece at all. *De Stijl* had not been founded as a movement and was therefore far from complete. The purely abstract vocabulary of form that was being propagated still had to be developed.

Mondrian's path towards abstraction was typical.[13] After some tentative endeavours to adapt current artistic developments, he received his significant impetus from Cubism. Until then he had tried his hand at Pointillism and Symbolism, with landscapes as his preferred subject.[14] Having learnt about the works and objectives of Cubism through a painter called Kickert, Mondrian embarked on a journey that would take him from abstract depiction to complete abstraction.[15]

In 1917, when Mondrian began to publish his fundamental theory on "Neo-Plasticism in Art",[16] the important steps had already been taken. With entire series of paintings on subjects that had occupied his mind for a long time – such as the sea and trees – the artist became increasingly radical and moved further and further away from representational art. His most important method was a schematic approach in which artistic shapes became more and more independent. The *Church Tower at Domburg*, for example (p. 30), had a certain heavy blockiness and linear straightness about it, so that it was particularly suitable for this purpose. Domberg was a little town in the Dutch province of Zeeland where Mondrian belonged to an artists' colony for a while.[17] As early as 1910/11, Mondrian felt inspired by the style of the Cubists and began to see the surrounding Zeeland architecture as an intricate pattern of juxtaposed and interpenetrating lines and colour fields. The reddish shape of the tower complements the green-blue of the sky, providing a striking colour contrast that would have been unusual for Cubism. The windows and doors of the building have turned into planes. They seem like holes within a static structure. The overall shape is determined by a small number of characteristic lines, so that we can discern the different floors and their architecture – an architecture whose planes correspond closely to the sharp, rugged contours of the atmospheric strata in the painting. Forming a mosaic of irregular, jagged planes, sometimes loose and sometimes dense, they fill the area on either side of the church tower.

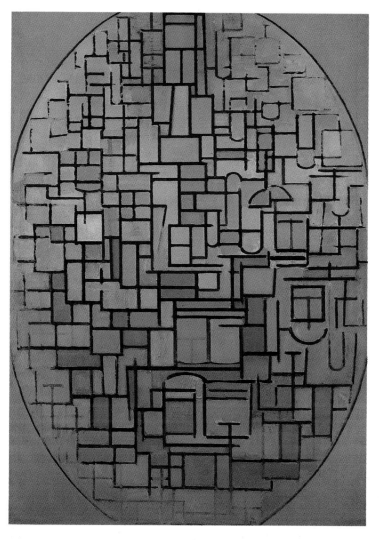

Piet Mondrian

Composition in Oval (Tableau III), 1914
Compositie in ovaal (Tableau III)
Oil on canvas, 140 x 101 cm
Stedelijk Museum, Amsterdam

Piet Mondrian

Composition in Oval, 1914
Compositie in ovaal
Oil on canvas, 113 x 84.5 cm
Gemeentemuseum, The Hague

*Mondrian based this composition on a view from
his studio window in Paris.*

The method of establishing a correspondence between the planes of an object and those of the background had already become a principle of artistic modelling in Cubism and was now taken over partly by Mondrian. A few years later he achieved complete abstraction (p. 33). If we did not know anything about the genesis of this painting and that these shapes were gleaned from a schematic depiction of a church tower, we would not recognize their provenance in reality. There is no longer any power of association. The pink planes, which are imitations of the lighter and more shady portions of the brickwork, have turned white-yellow, beige and reddish, partly surrounded by straight lines and adding up to rectangular structures. A small number of rounded lines still remind us of the church's doors and windows. However, they have all lost their original significance and have spread out quite arbitrarily over the whole area of the painting. Shape has become autonomous and devoid of any representational character.

However, this path towards the abstract, which Mondrian saw and formulated as a logical development and indeed aim of Cubism, was a misunderstanding. The Cubists, led by Picasso and Braque, never wanted total abstraction. Such a thought would have been completely alien to their whole way of thinking and their artistic ideas.[18] Rather, just like Mondrian, the Cubists wanted to achieve the autonomy of depiction in art. But it was precisely in order to show this autonomy that the Cubists never completely abandoned the link between depiction and the depicted subject. By decomposing the lines and colour configurations of representational art, they demonstrated the arbitrariness of all attempts to reproduce reality and showed how a totally new world of images could be created if the artist abandoned the idea of merely rendering what he could see with his eyes. However, this would have been impossible without the presence of representational forms in their art. This approach continued throughout the different phases of Cubism, starting with the first analysis of shapes (1907/08 to c. 1909/10), followed by Analytical Cubism (c. 1910 to 1912), where compositional structures were split up and almost atomized, and finally Synthetic Cubism (c. 1912 to 1914), where new artistic methods and techniques yielded new structures. In particular, this was true where logic was turned into its opposite. For divergences can only be perceived if they are recognized as such. However, this was not Mondrian's approach.

"I gradually realized," he wrote later, "that Cubism did not accept the logical consequences of its own discoveries; it did not develop abstraction to its utmost consequence, the expression of pure truth."[19] This central thought shows the whole difference between Mondrian and Cubism. Cubist painters were profoundly convinced that it was questionable whether our perception of reality could ever attain the absolute. This, however, was precisely Mondrian's aim. He decided that reality was something absolute that lay behind the chance phenomena of this world, while Cubists painted the relativity of all things, which they emphasized again and again in their intricate art. Mondrian, on the other hand, maintained that "the manifestation of natural forms

Georges Braque

Still Life with Harp and Violin, 1911
Nature morte harpe et violon
Oil on canvas, 116 x 81 cm
Kunstsammlung Nordrhein-Westfalen,
Düsseldorf

Piet Mondrian

Composition No. 6, 1914
Compositie Nr. 6
Oil on canvas, 88 x 61 cm
Gemeentemuseum, The Hague

Piet Mondrian

The Red Tree, 1908
De rode boom
Oil on canvas, 70 x 99 cm
Gemeentemuseum, The Hague

changes, but reality remains constant."[20] Obviously, someone with this kind of philosophy could never accept that the artistic endeavours of Cubism, with their emphasis on chance and their calculated demonstration of arbitrariness, could possibly yield satisfactory results.

But although Mondrian's paintings of 1914 (pp. 33 and 34) were undoubtedly an important step towards pure abstraction, they did not actually achieve it. Mondrian, who had moved to Paris at the beginning of the decade, was suddenly trapped in the Netherlands on a visit to his parents when the First World War broke out. In 1916, cut off from the Parisian world of art and thrown back to provincialism in his creative urges, he met an artist whose work inspired him to overcome Cubism: Bart van der Leck. It was only a very brief encounter, but one that was to influence him quite considerably.[21] For the first time Mondrian saw a system of abstract depiction that only knew straight lines, primary colours and shades of black, grey and white, as well as clearly delineated planes. Van der Leck's painting *Composition 1916 No. 4* (p. 40) was enthusiastically hailed by a newly formed artists' circle of spiritual kinsmen, which included Mondrian, van Doesburg and Huszár.[22]

Piet Mondrian

The Grey Tree, 1912
De grijze boom
Oil on canvas, 78.5 x 107.5 cm
Gemeentemuseum, The Hague

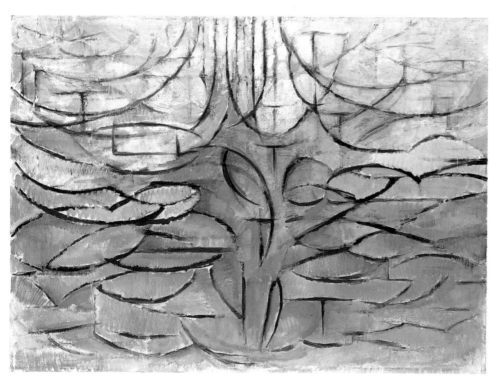

Piet Mondrian

Blossoming Apple Tree, 1912
De bloeiende appelboom
Oil on canvas, 78 x 106 cm
Gemeentemuseum, The Hague

In these and other paintings of the same period, especially his compositions of 1917, abstraction does indeed seem to have reached a position of autonomy, and the artist's restriction to elements of plasticity seems to be radical and consistent. However, it would be a fallacy to think of these paintings as totally autonomous and purely intellectual constructs. This is true of Mondrian's and van Doesburg's later paintings of the Twenties. Both *Composition 1917 No. 3*, of which he painted two variants, and *Composition 1916 No. 4* are merely further developments of totally non-abstract works (pp. 40, 42 and 43).[23] Van der Leck's painting of 1916 was based on studies of a mine that he had inspected and drawn during a journey to Spain and Algeria in 1914 (pp. 38 and 39), and his composition of 1917 derived its inspiration from a picture of workers pouring out of a factory after their day's labour. For both abstract paintings van der Leck created a repertoire of shapes – cycles of studies that included several sheets each time. Bringing about the utmost reduction of shapes and confining himself to primary colours, he achieved total abstraction.

The subject of his so-called *Mine Triptych* (p. 40) was a series of studies of a colliery (p. 38). The blue and red lines and the black oblique lines are remnants of a complicated landscape and formation of rocks that had been rendered more and more two-dimensional in his preliminary studies (pp. 38 and 39). The same system can be found in *Composition 1917 No. 3* (p. 42), which is also referred to as *Geometrical Composition* in the relevant literature.[24] The red lines at the top mark the walls of a factory, the black ones its windows, the black and blue lines at the

Bart van der Leck

Study of a Mine in Spain, 1914
Mijntekening
Pencil and watercolour, 214 x 134 cm
Rijksmuseum Kröller-Müller, Otterlo

From April 11th to July 1st, 1914, the artist travelled to Spain and Algeria to inspect branches of the Dutch Müller group of companies. During his journey he made 100 drawings and watercolours. His large abstract Mine Triptych *was based on some of them. The study shown here was used for the left-hand side panel (p. 40).*

Bart van der Leck

Four studies for the painting *Composition 1916 No. 4* (Mine Triptych), 1916
Vier studies voor "Mijntriptiek"
Gouache, 12.7 x 13.3; 12.9 x 13; 12.4 x 12.8; 13.2 x 13 cm
Rijksmuseum Kröller-Müller, Otterlo

In these studies Bart van der Leck developed the abstract composition of the central panel of his Mine Triptych, *which was based on his 1914 series of sketches, drawn during a trip to Spain and Algeria. His starting point was a drawing that shows the entrance of the mine in a rocky landscape. The central motif of the entrance, with its black edges and the road that leads diagonally towards it, recurs as a system of black lines*

bottom are abstract representations of the workers' bodies, while the yellow pins indicate their heads and limbs. This shows that van der Leck's imagery is still very much based on the real world, which remains the starting point and the reference point of all abstraction. His series of preliminary studies, which always preceded his compositions, shows the principle very clearly, regardless of the motifs that served as the starting points of his paintings. His increasingly systematic limitation to borderlines always yielded seemingly abstract compositions.

The obvious attractiveness of van der Leck's works lay not so much in his method, but in the quality of his concentration on shapes that were consistently pure and geometrical, as well as his restriction to primary colours. His *Dock Work* (p. 41), also painted in 1916, is concerned not so much with geometrical and linear reduction as schematic planes – a stylistic method that had long been in use in poster art. This is hardly surprising when we consider that, in 1915, van der Leck had designed posters for Müller & Co.'s Batavia line and that he was in fact some kind of company artist for this enterprise. For several years he had been specially sponsored by the owner of the company, Mrs. Kröller-Müller, who was also the co-founder of a museum in Otterloo, named after her. He carried out a number of different jobs for Müller & Co., including posters, stained glass windows and mosaics for buidings of the company.[25]

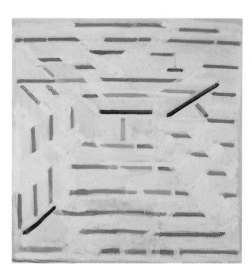

and planes which are increasingly reduced to mere lines. A similar stylization of forms can be seen in the various parts of the rocky landscape which become restless layers of rectangles, then zig-zags and finally also lines. The use of primary colours follows the same principle of increasingly abstract and schematic forms of nature. Brown, yellow-beige and shady blue portions of the rocks are rendered more and more

colourful. The final result is a completely abstract conglomeration of horizontal, vertical and diagonal lines against a white background.

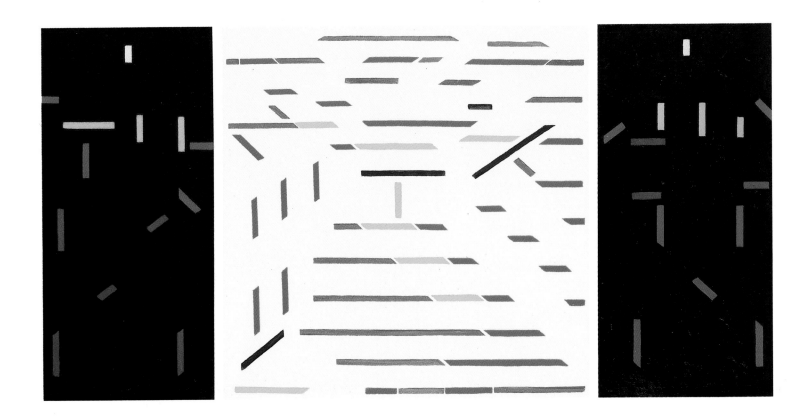

Bart van der Leck

Composition 1916 No. 4 (Mine Triptych), 1916
Compositie 1916–4 (Mijntriptiek)
Oil on canvas, 110 x 220 cm
Centre panel: 110 x 110 cm
Side panels: 110 x 55 cm each
Gemeentemuseum, The Hague
On loan from the Rijksdienst Beeldende Kunst

We can easily see how advertising had influenced the artist: the emphasis on the conciseness of motifs, a degree of stylization that can be easily remembered and the conscious use of bright colours to evoke certain signals. *Dock Work* gave Mondrian an excellent opportunity to study the specific character of colours, their different spatial weights, their emotional appeal in conjunction with shapes aimed entirely at two-dimensional rendering, and the way in which all these elements combine to lend a painting a peculiar effect no longer connected with the motif of nature, but with an artistic character of its own. In this way van der Leck developed a colour system that he had taken over from another painter – Vincent van Gogh. Van Gogh's later paintings are characterized by the use of virtually unbroken primary colours dominating large sections of his compositions.[26] However, he restricted himself to non-abstract depiction. Blue is only ever used for blue objects, and the same is true for red and yellow.

One key painting which shows van Gogh's influence on van der Leck is *The Storm* (p. 41), also painted in 1916. It shows a traditional motif of Dutch art – a scene from the life of fisherfolk. Standing on the seashore are two fisherwomen awaiting the return of a boat. The boat can be seen in an abstract form on a heavy, tempestuous sea in the top left-hand corner. Despite this stylization, the painting is still consistently realistic, especially in its use of colour. The beach is yellow, the sea is blue, the sails are red, and the clothes of the women are black and blue – not just for purely compositional reasons, but as a correct rendering of traditional Scheveningen costumes.[27]

Bart van der Leck

Dock Work, 1916
Havenarbeid
Oil on canvas, 89 x 240 cm
Rijksmuseum Kröller-Müller, Otterlo

Bart van der Leck

The Storm, 1916
De storm
Oil on canvas, 118 x 59 cm
Rijksmuseum Kröller-Müller, Otterlo

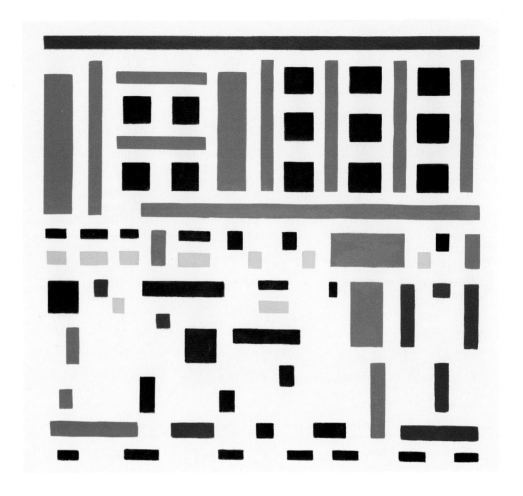

This necessity of clear contrasts, which enhanced the representational meaning in such a stylized painting, also explains the use of pure white for the faces. It is an element that anticipates further developments, for these white planes seem like holes in the composition. It gives the colours a certain spatial character in *Dock Work* (p. 41), a quality that became a whole principle and gave Mondrian his important inspiration to paint compositions of colours and shapes independently of real-life subjects, bringing about a stable balance between space and plane; a balance that negated or even superseded any spatial illusions. In his endeavour to move away from Cubism Mondrian was inspired by van der Leck, a development that can also be seen in his almost geometrical linearity and tendency towards bright colours. But van der Leck also learnt from Mondrian. The linear geometrization of his compositions at the end of 1916 and the subsequent years, as well as their entire conception, can be seen as a combination of Mondrian's strict linearity, the planar effect derived from the two-dimensional nature of posters and the use of primary colours.

And so it was not only the example of Cubism that influenced the development of *De Stijl*, but also a type of imagery that was deeply rooted in applied art – and in the works of van Gogh.

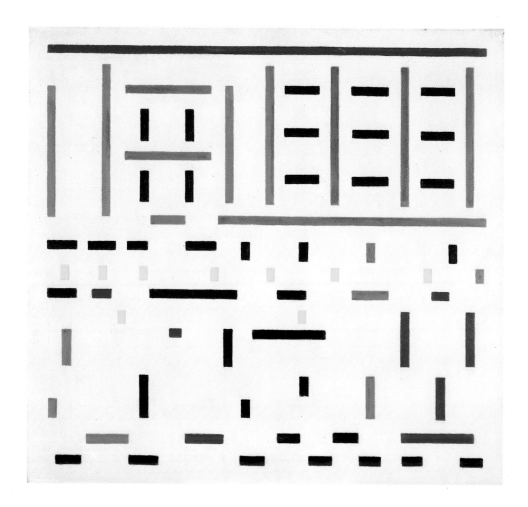

Bart van der Leck

Composition 1917 No. 4
(End of Day at the Factory), 1917
Compositie 1917–4 (Uitgaan van de fabriek)
Oil on canvas, 94 x 100 cm
Rijksmuseum Kröller-Müller, Otterlo

Unless we take account of these influences, we cannot fully understand the journey towards pure abstraction in *De Stijl*. Although the large number of new artistic movements at the end of the 1910s and 20s had made a profound impression on *De Stijl* artists, they did not affect the definition of their own style. Vantongerloo is a case in point. Having emigrated from Belgium to the Netherlands at the outbreak of the First World War, he had displayed works at his first exhibitions in The Hague which were inspired by Post-Impressionists, and particularly van Gogh.[28] Through his acquaintance with another Belgian painter in exile, Jules Schmalzigaug, he began to be influenced by Italian Futurism.[29] Futurists were apparently trying to find suitable artistic ways of expressing the new realities of our modern world, above all the dynamics of the machine age and its central dimensions of time and speed.[30] Vantongerloo's works of 1916 to 1917/18 were influenced by Futurism. He tried to combine the dissolution of form as developed by Pointillists and Impressionists with the dynamic grid patterns of the Futurists. It was only through the example of *De Stijl*, which he joined in 1918, that Vantongerloo adopted the pure abstraction of geometrical forms, defined by strict right angles and bright, expressive colours.

Theo van Doesburg

Self-Portrait (?), 1915
Zelfportret(?)
Pastel, 16 x 11.5 cm
Rijksdienst Beeldende Kunst, The Hague

Theo van Doesburg

Heroic Movement, 1916
Heroïsche beweging
Oil on canvas, 136 x 110.5 cm
Rijksdienst Beeldende Kunst, The Hague

Van Doesburg, the magazine's editor-in-chief and driving force behind the *De Stijl* movement, had developed in a similar way: for a number of years he had already made a name for himself with articles on art in different publications, and he had been influenced by van Gogh, Expressionism and the Italian Futurists.[31] A portrait of 1915 (above left) – probably a self-portrait – which he himself described as "expressionistic-theosophical" uses two-dimensional stylization with brightly colourful contrasts as a method of expressing his own personal mood as well as his philosophical and ideological state of mind. One of his major works of 1916, called *Heroic Movement* (above right) is already an almost totally abstract painting and shows how his oeuvre at that time was dominated by this fusion of German and Italian ideas. Dynamism is coupled with a formalism of geometrical composition that imposes a certain peacefulness and achieves a balance between extremes. This is because the structure of the painting was based on a linear grid pattern. But the picture only seems to be purely abstract. Behind it there is a drawing of a moving male figure, transformed and rendered independent through its stylization. The figure expresses, as far as we know, van Doesburg's inner and outer circumstances in a period of his life which he perceived as heroic. Also, the style of the picture is very close to that of Janus de Winter, a painter whom van Doesburg admired very much at the time.[32]

Van Doesburg was already familiar with Mondrian's latest works, especially his *Sea* paintings. In his publications he particularly mentioned Mondrian's studies and compositions of 1915. However, there is no evidence of any direct influence at this stage. And even his first

Theo van Doesburg

Card Players, 1916–1917
De kaartspelers
Tempera on canvas, 117 x 147 cm
Rijksdienst Beeldende Kunst, The Hague

meeting with Mondrian and the theosophist Schoenmaker at the Laren artists' colony in 1916, when they apparently discussed their artistic ideals, merely led to collaboration between the two painters, who expressed their wish to work together on a new magazine, planned by van Doesburg.[33]

Van Doesburg's contact with Vilmos Huszár, a naturalized Hungarian who had come to live in the Netherlands, was far more important. Unfortunately, Huszár's paintings are now lost and only available in the form of old black-and-white photographs of poor quality. They show that Huszár had been influenced by Symbolism and the works of van Gogh. Van Doesburg was so enthusiastic about Huszár's *Schilderij in geel* (Painting in Yellow) that he decided to buy it.[34] (It was probably destroyed during the bombing of Rotterdam in the Second World War.) The painting was totally monochrome and in yellow, van Gogh's favourite colour, and consisted of restless, interlocking geometrical planes. This mixture of curved lines as an expression of dynamic elements and geometrically static rigidity showed the influence of paintings of the Italian Futurist Gino Severini. (It is therefore hardly surprising that a painting of Severini was published as a Futurist work par excellence in the second issue of *De Stijl*, together with a theoretical article by the same artist.) This mixture of post-Impressionist and Futurist ideas, which also spoke to Vantongerloo, helped van Doesburg a great deal. Inspired also by the example of Cézanne and his postulate that artistic expression should be reduced to basic geometrical artistic elements, van Doesburg reached an intermediate stage, reflected in his major work of this period, a painting called *Card Players*: it is a composition

45

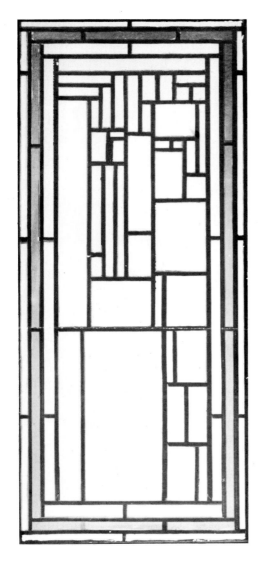

Vilmos Huszár

Girl, 1916
Meisje
Draft for a stained glass composition, now lost

Theo van Doesburg

Woman's Head, 1917
Vrouwekop
Stained glass, 39 x 26 cm
Rijksdienst Beeldende Kunst, The Hague

that consists entirely of colour planes which add up to geometrically stylized human figures, with an intricate mixture of triangles, rectangles and a small number of rounded shapes. The planar character of the playing cards became a basic principle for the rendering of the figures. However, although this makes the figures appear abstract, it is not in itself abstract art. Van Doesburg received his important impetus from quite a different area, with an entirely different system of forms: applied art. Unlike Bart van der Leck, he did not draw his inspiration from the logic of poster-like effects, but from ornamental principles.

His attention was drawn to ornamentation when he was commissioned to design stained glass windows – something which had also influenced van der Leck. In 1916 van Doesburg had met not only Mondrian, Huszár and van der Leck, but also Oud and Wils, the other artists who were instrumental in founding *De Stijl*. Oud had helped van Doesburg to obtain orders for stained glass windows in private houses which the architect had built for various patrons.[35] Van Doesburg's first works were similar to Huszár's of the same period. They were schematic depictions of figures, e.g. his *Card Players*. It is therefore plausible to assume that this method was influenced by stained glass windows. Huszár and van Doesburg then received an important impulse from the perfect abstraction in van der Leck's *Mine Triptych* (p. 40). Their stained glass windows subsequently changed radically and became more progressive than previous ones. However, van der Leck's example does not explain the essential character of these windows. Huszár's works cannot really be adequately judged any longer, since most of them are only available to us in the form of black and white photographs, though they are very similar in structure to his *Composition with White Head* of 1917 (p. 48). Like Bart van der Leck, Huszár's methods were stylization, the geometrization of real-life figures and their treatment as something independent. Thus he managed to paint purely abstract pictures whose only link with the original subjects was associative.

Van Doesburg then created his *Woman's Head* (p. 47), a stained glass window that was modelled on Huszár's. This artistic breakthrough was directly based on Huszár's draft for a glass window, and we know from a letter from van Doesburg that it was the abstraction of a portrait of his girl friend Helena Milius: "I have designed a portrait of Helena in stained glass! It makes the Middle Ages seem completely useless! Only a few hours later I'm still trembling, and even now I have tears running down my cheeks when I look at the study. It is the most beautiful thing I've ever made in stained glass."[36]

These words seem rather exuberant to us now, and we find the painter's enthusiasm difficult to follow, considering that it was a second-hand achievement. However, it meant a lot to van Doesburg. It helped him to discover the important *De Stijl* principle for himself – an autonomous composition with rectangular planes, arranged horizontally and vertically. But it was still no more abstract than the paintings of van der Leck or Huszár of the same period.

46

Vilmos Huszár

Composition with White Head, 1917
Compositie met witte kop
Oil on wood, 50.7 x 45 cm
Gemeentemuseum, The Hague

Another draft for a stained glass window, however, shows everything that was typical of *De Stijl*: autonomous colours, lines and planes, a pure play of weights and the significance of painterly elements (p. 51). The stained glass itself has been lost since then, but we do know the circumstances of its creation and where it was originally installed. It was a window at *Allegonda*, a beach villa, redecorated by Oud, in the seaside resort of Katwijk aan Zee. We can get a clear idea of the structure of this abstract composition if we compare the coloured study and the construction design for the lead frame (p. 50). What seems at first sight rather confusing in the actual line drawing, and extremely complex and varied in the colour draft, can be reduced to a few variations of shapes: the entire picture consists of three narrow horizontal bands, each of which has been subdivided into vertically stacked planes. Yet this confusing abundance looks more complicated than it really is, as van Doesburg created several basic grid patterns of rectangles which he spread across the picture by repeating them in different

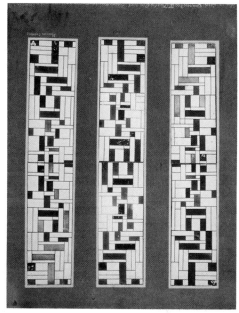

Theo van Doesburg

Abstraction of Card Players,
Composition IX, 1917
*Abstractie doorbeelding "De kaartspelers",
Compositie IX*
Oil on canvas, 116 x 116 cm
Gemeentemuseum, The Hague

Theo van Doesburg

Stained Glass Composition IV, triptych for the
staircase at the house of the notary J. de Lange,
Alkmaar, 1917
Glas-in-loodcompositie IV, Triptiek
Stained glass windows, 286.5 x 56.6 cm each
Rijksdienst Beeldende Kunst, The Hague

places, changing their direction, turning them upside down, etc. This
does indeed make for total abstraction, without any imitation of realistic
subjects; nor was it derived from any existing pattern.[37]

Nevertheless, the structure of the picture was not new, but one of the
oldest in fine art altogether. It has always been a typical feature of
ornamental art that identical motifs are turned around or upside down
and then arranged horizontally or distributed vertically. Often these
motifs are almost or indeed completely abstract. The deliberate asym-
metry in van Doesburg's composition – a basic principle in *De Stijl* art –
is certainly no indication of a break with the ornamental principle, for
there are plenty of examples of asymmetrical ornaments and ornamental decorations in the history of art.[38]

Theo van Doesburg

Preliminary sketch for Stained Glass
Composition V, 1917–1918
Ontwerptekening voor glas-in-loodcompositie V
Phototype, 108 x 66 cm
Rijksdienst Beeldende Kunst, The Hague

Van Doesburg himself felt that, with this composition, he had ful-filled his ideal of a pure configuration of tones, gleaned from the musical structures of Bach. However, this should not blind us to the fact that, although he always followed examples, he was in fact applying a traditional idea – the principle of ornamentation. But this pattern had now become autonomous, and the repetition and variation of motifs was deliberately broken in a number of places in order to overcome it. Nevertheless, there is still an overall structure. Also, the principle of ornamental forms seemed an obvious solution because it was such a common method in the design of stained glass windows. The large windows at *Villa Lange* of 1917 (p. 49), which have been preserved intact, are also based on ornamental structures. Undoubtedly, Huszár and van Doesburg were also influenced by the example of Viennese applied art at the turn of the century, with its ornamental variation of conventional groups of motifs.[39]

Van Doesburg's important step towards *De Stijl* in 1917 can there-fore be understood as a fusion of different artistic innovations of his time with varying degrees of modernness – a synthesis that was achieved by the principle of ornamentation. In his *Abstraction of Card Players* of 1917 (p. 49) van Doesburg translated his newly acquired vocabulary of form into the medium of the canvas. Although it is based on the schematic rendering of existing shapes again, it is now combined with a new insight into the specific weight of the various tone values of colours – including black, white and grey - vis-à-vis the expressive forcefulness of rectangular shapes. Clusters of small rectangles, sur-rounded by lines, are reminiscent of the decorative grid patterns of sketches and suggest depth. They compete with the powerful areas of black, and the whole picture is given a confusingly iridescent spatial effect by the sparing but extremely effective use of blue and grey rectangles. In this way the artist achieves the harmonization of opposing principles, because each one of them – including elementary shapes, primary colours and colourless planes – has its own, specific character which is not easily convertible. Any correspondence therefore needs to be constructed specially.

This shows that the complexity of *De Stijl*'s vocabulary of form is due to a process which covers a great diversity of highly complex traditions. That the editor of *De Stijl* was very much aware of this development can be seen in the two large stained glass windows of his *Great Pastoral Scene*, which he designed for the Drachten School of Agriculture in 1921. Although van Doesburg's final, window-sized draft was not purely abstract, he had it installed in his studio while he was staying in Weimar in 1922. In this way van Doesburg gave special programmatic emphasis to one of the basic tenets of his most important propaganda campaigns undertaken on behalf of *De Stijl*.

Indeed this stained glass window, which is the stylization of actual objects, contains everything that had become important in the basic principles of *De Stijl*'s vocabulary of form. To suit the setting of the window, some typical agricultural activities are represented by abstract

Theo van Doesburg

Colour draft for Stained Glass
Composition V,
for the *Villa Allegonda*,
Katwijk aan Zee, 1918
*Kleurontwerp voor glas-in-
loodcompositie V*
Gouache, 85.5 x 50 cm
Vereinigung Zürcher Kunst-
freunde, Kunsthaus Zürich

Vincent van Gogh

The Sower, 1889–1890
De zaaier
Oil on canvas, 80.8 x 66 cm
Stavros S. Niarchos Collection, London

Theo van Doesburg

Sketches and studies for his *"Great Pastoral Scene"*, 1921
Schetsontwerpen voor "Grote Pastorale"
Pencil, ink and watercolour on paper
Rijksdienst Beeldende Kunst, The Hague

Van Doesburg's series of studies of his Great Pastoral Scene *in Drachten and his colour draft for the* Small Pastoral Scene *at the same place give a good idea of the artist's process of abstraction. The changing figure of the sower shows, step by step, the process of an increasingly schematic and geometrical rendering of the relevant shape. The figure was based on van Gogh's famous painting* The Sower. *Van Doesburg first produced a copy of the figure. He then placed a sketchy draft right next to it as a first attempt to produce a straightened and stylized version of it. In his subsequent sketches he decomposed the figure into individual planes, which he understood as structures with triangles and rectangles. The final version was a shape consisting of black and white planes, and the last stage was a typical* De Stijl *composition of primary colours and colourless planes.*

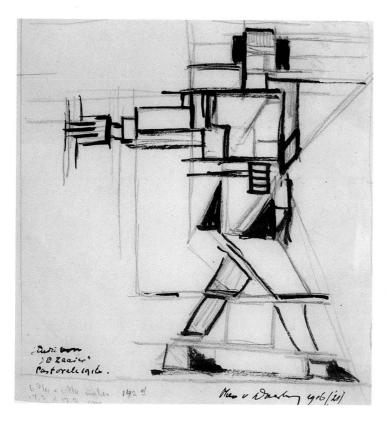

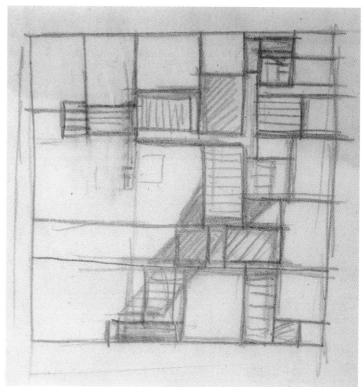

Theo and Nelly van Doesburg, together with
Harry Scheibe at van Doesburg's studio in
Weimar, in February 1922. On the right are the
artist's four final drafts for his stained glass composition The Great Pastoral Scene.

Theo van Doesburg

Colour draft for the *"Great Pastoral Scene"*
Kleurontwerp voor "Grote Pastorale"
Pencil, ink and watercolour on paper
Rijksdienst Beeldende Kunst, The Hague

*The two-part stained glass window in the stair-
well of the Drachten School of Agriculture (illustration opposite) shows four typical activities in
the life of a farmer. During renovation work the
two panels were unfortunately changed round,
thus disturbing the cyclical relationship which
van Doesburg wanted to emphasize with the arrangement of his figures. The right-hand side
was originally on the left and vice versa. The figures were related to each other in a sequence
that expressed an infinite process.*

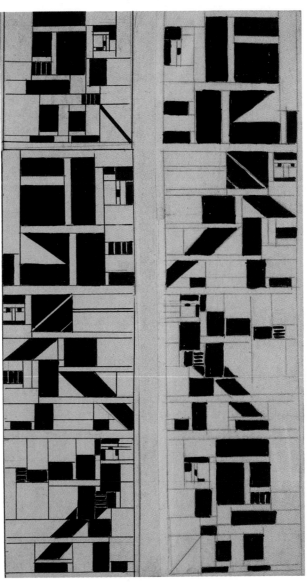

54

Theo van Doesburg

Great Pastoral Scene, 1921–1922
Grote pastorale
Stained glass windows,
300 x 70 cm each
School of Agriculture, Drachten

figures, still recognizable as such. This was done in the same way as Bart van der Leck's method of abstract geometrical composition.

However, the figures, which are in primary colours, are remodelled versions of several patterns by van Gogh, whom the *De Stijl* artists regarded as one the founders of modern art.[40] Van Doesburg's stylization of van Gogh's *Sower* is a good example of how he went about it and how he produced a unique combination of applied art, decorative principles, traditions, enthusiasm for van Gogh and the development of his own artistic direction.[41] The depiction of agricultural activities as a cycle is very old and has certainly not been toned down here by the cosmological references implied in the four seasons.[42]

This shows another way in which *De Stijl* artists made creative use of traditions. They used forms – so-called *pathetic formulae* – that had been handed down as meaningful metaphors.[43] Van Doesburg's *Card Players* (p. 45), for example, do not fill the whole canvas, but only a plane defined by a pointed arch, quite probably a deliberate reminder of ecclesiastic forms common in church architecture. Ecclesiastic conventions also inspired important works of van der Leck and Vantongerloo (pp. 38, 40 and 57). Their triptychs are reflections of three-part altarpieces that can be closed and opened. Although the triptych had long become secularized,[44] it had retained its value as a pathetic formula which was used quite deliberately by Vantongerloo. While closed, like an altar on a weekday, the work appears to be no more than an abstract composition of painted lines and colours. When it is open, we can see an abstract, yet plastic and therefore formally enhanced composition, between two abstract, rectangular paintings. The dark sides turn light towards the middle of the painting – a device that served as a reversal strategy in Bart van der Leck's art, whereas Georges Vantongerloo intended it as an abstract revelation. When his own triptych is opened, the side panels with their mixed tones reveal a composition consisting of primary colours and set against pure shapes. The two views are joined together by a green plane.[45]

This shows that before *De Stijl* artists took an interest in avant-garde – the most modern movement at the time – they defined their concrete artistic intentions to a large extent on the basis of traditional forms. The elementary features of *De Stijl* reflect the creative use of ancient artistic principles, such as ornamentation and stylization in applied art.

Paradoxically, therefore, tradition itself became an instrument for completely overcoming tradition, and the process in which this happened was propounded with almost messianic zeal.

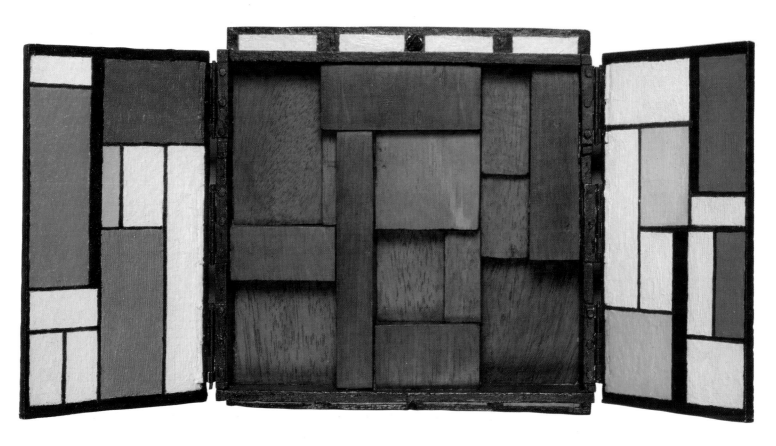

Georges Vantongerloo

Triptych, 1921
triptyque
Painted wooden blocks on wood,
13 x 13 cm (closed), 13 x 26 cm (open)
Private collection

Theo van Doesburg

Counter-Composition V, 1924
Contra-compositie V
Oil on canvas, 100 x 100 cm
Stedelijk Museum, Amsterdam

4: The Ideal as Art

But despite its radically new and purely abstract vocabulary of form in fine art, *De Stijl* was by no means a special case in the history of so-called classical Modernism. Nor was it special simply because it was proclaimed with such zeal, or because its ideas and forms were propagated in manifestoes, or even because it had its own magazine.

There was already a long history of art magazines, and a group around a magazine was nothing new either. It was the beginning of the age of mass media, and so journals of this kind were rather a typical feature of this period.[46] Nor was there anything unique in the fact that the movement had not yet developed its full potential and that its members derived encouragement from this very handicap. Such an attitude was even more noticeable in Futurism, the movement that had inspired *De Stijl* so much. When Marinetti published the first Futurist manifesto in the Parisian *Le Figaro* in 1909, there was no Futurist art or Futurist artists. (The term was therefore consistent and genuine, because the group and the artistic movement only came into being afterwards.)[47]

In this sense *De Stijl* was very typical of its time. And so was the fundamental philosophy of the movement and the vocabulary of form which its artists were aiming to define. The most important key to an understanding of the founders of *De Stijl* can be found in Mondrian's article *Neo-Plasticism in Painting*, published in the first issue of the magazine. (The essay also gave the movement the name *Neo-Plasticism*, a direct translation of the Dutch "nieuwe beelding"). In his article Mondrian defined the new artistic movement as more than a new individual style of spiritual kinsmen, but something that went much further and was far more significant: it was to be an expression of a new, ideal world.

Though aimed at the future, the idea was typical of the age. According to Mondrian, modern man enjoyed a degree of spiritual independence that was unprecedented, and he therefore perceived life differently from his predecessors. In art this new perception was thought to be paralleled by the central significance of our sense of beauty, a sense that was cosmic and universal and therefore transcended all individual sensations which might disturb the ideal state. As a result, any form of art that was aimed at the ideal future was necessarily seen as anti-individualistic and universalist. Borrowings from nature, which were characteristic of traditional art, were bound to be anti-universalist, because all forms of nature were marked by individualism. For the sake of its totally universal aim Neo-Plasticism therefore necessarily had to be abstract.

After all, pure art, said Mondrian, was an expression of pure spirit. An art that aimed at pure beauty necessarily had to use pure forms. It was a postulate that followed logically from the basic premises of history and art. Although art was always striving for the absolute, it could only manifest itself within time. This was the phenomenon of style. Style in painting was therefore determined by a universal content aimed at the absolute and by its manifestation in time. It followed further that to achieve this absolute intention, the best possible style was the one

Piet Mondrian

Self-Portrait, 1918
Zelfportret
Oil on canvas, 88 x 71 cm
Gemeentemuseum, The Hague

Piet Mondrian

Lozenge with Ochre and Grey Planes, 1919
Ruit met vlakken in oker en grijs
Oil on canvas, 84 cm diagonally
Rijksmuseum Kröller-Müller, Otterlo

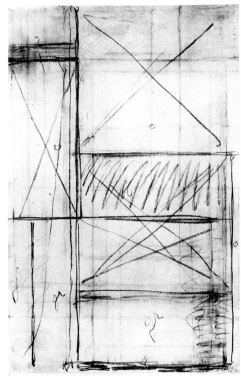

Piet Mondrian

Composition I with Red, Yellow and Blue, 1921
Compositie I met rood, geel en blauw
Oil on canvas, 103 x 100 cm
Gemeentemuseum, The Hague

Piet Mondrian

Sketch for *"Tableau I"*
Schetsontwerp voor "Tableau I"
Charcoal on paper, 96 x 62 cm
The Pace Gallery, New York

where "the individual was most strongly subject to the universal."[48] The inherent contradiction in this statement was fundamental to Neo-Plasticism, and as style is a phenomenon in time and therefore always subject to the individual, Mondrian concluded: "The universal in style must be expressed by the individual, i.e. the way in which style is formed." Consequently, an art that was conscious of its real task could only aim at the universal, the absolute and the things that transcended the individual. As a result, it had to use methods that were universal and abstract, that is, elementary.

Mondrian's ideas of the calling of art and the principles governing its manifestations were entirely based on the general concept of *style* that prevailed at the time.

Ever since Alois Riegl's theory of *Artistic Intention,* art historians had believed that a given vocabulary of form which was common to a given geographical area or artistic period also expressed the artistic intentions of that area or period. Thus the word *style* was used as a concept which lent quasi-scientific objectivity to an examination and understanding of art, without the prejudiced viewpoint of one's own time. In fact, it was even believed that so-called basic concepts in art

Piet Mondrian

Tableau I, 1921
Tableau I
Oil on canvas, 96.5 x 60.5 cm
Museum Ludwig, Cologne

Piet Mondrian

Composition with Colour Planes No. 3, 1917
Compositie met kleurvlakjes nr. 3
Oil on canvas, 48 x 61 cm
Gemeentemuseum, The Hague

history could be derived in this way.[49] The development of these ideas led many artists to study the phenomenon of *style*, ranging from Gottfried Semper, the architect and theoretician of Historicism, to Hendrikus Peter Berlage, the founding father of modern Dutch architecture who, characteristically, had written a monograph titled *Thoughts on Style* in 1905.[50]

So it was not mere chance but historical consistency that led the newly formed group around Theo van Doesburg and Piet Mondrian to call their mouthpiece *De Stijl*.[51]

Other aspects that were typical of the time were the artists' all-embracing claim of absolute validity, the utopian aim of their endeavours and their detailed theoretical reasons, as well as the demand that tradition should be overcome and a new, abstract vocabulary of form should be created. When *De Stijl* was founded, individual artists

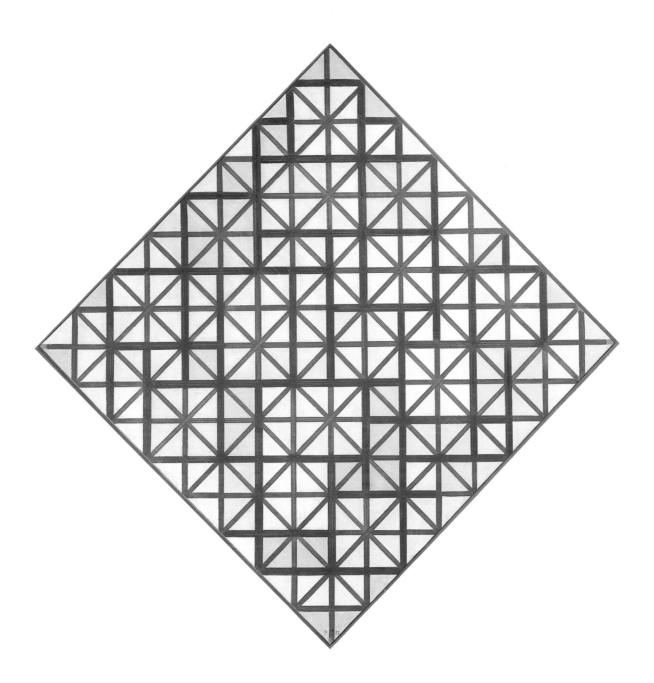

Piet Mondrian

Lozenge with Grey Lines, 1918
Ruit met grijze lijnen
Oil on canvas, 121 cm diagonally
Gemeentemuseum, The Hague

and whole groups of artists had already experimented with abstraction and had offered their theoretical justifications, such as Wassily Kandinsky with his essay on *On the Spiritual in Art*, published in 1912.[52] This influenced the birth of *De Stijl* and helps us to understand it as a special case of abstract art. *De Stijl* emerged as part of so-called Constructivism, a movement characterized by an extremely rational method of creating forms.[53] For *De Stijl* artists this rationalism followed logically from their utopian intention to achieve the absolute and to realize their ideal. Again, it was Mondrian who justified this most emphatically. The overall aim of art, as he proclaimed it, was simply the formation of pure objectivity and truth. He stated that, from an aesthetically subjective point of view, "beauty is truth" and concluded that "beauty is truth in the way it is perceived. And truth is the overall unity of opposites. If we are to find truth in beauty, then it must be found in it as an overall unity."[54]

Theo van Doesburg

Composition XVII, 1919
Compositie XVII
Oil on canvas, 50 x 50 cm
Gemeentemuseum, The Hague

This guiding principle determined the artistic language of the emerging *De Stijl* movement – at least in the early years. It enabled Mondrian to combine abstract composition with the use of elementary means in order to create beauty as a balance of relationships between opposites. He therefore began to use primary colours, shades of white, black and grey, as well as straight lines set at right angles (i.e. as horizontal or vertical lines) to balance out space versus time and rest versus movement in the relationship between different planes. Thus he achieved a concrete rendering of his ideal – absolute harmony. This is where the utopian function of art could be found. And once this ideal world had become real, art no longer had a right to exist.[55]

Mondrian's system of ideas and that of the other *De Stijl* artists was a combination of a certain philosophy and strictly rational artistic methods. In this sense it was certainly typical of the time. After all, it was not just the pioneers of *De Stijl* who were able to say, as did Mondrian: "The life of today's cultured person turns more and more away from nature; it is an increasingly abstract life."[56] The idea was shared by most avant-garde artists in the emerging industrial societies of the machine age. However, it was not seen as anything negative at first, but as something that had to be whole-heartedly affirmed and would help man

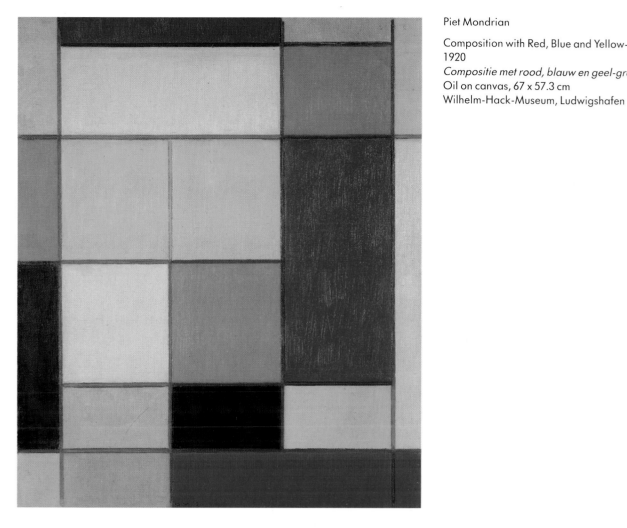

Piet Mondrian

Composition with Red, Blue and Yellow-Green, 1920
Compositie met rood, blauw en geel-groen
Oil on canvas, 67 x 57.3 cm
Wilhelm-Hack-Museum, Ludwigshafen

in his search for spiritual purity and ideal existence.[57] In fact, it is characteristic of the mechanization of this world that it reduced the abundance of individual phenomena to their general components and that it turns this process of abstraction into a basis for life.

That the fine arts responded to this historical process can be seen in the late 19th century when new methods of visual depiction were developed to capture the general concept of dynamics in all its purity, without embellishment. The photographic experiments of the Frenchman E.J. Marey and the American F.B. Gilbreth were quite typical. They used an ingenious technique to depict the process of movement in a static and totally abstract system of lines. Their photography was effective and influenced not only Futurism. Characteristically, the most highly developed of these motion photographs was the work of a production engineer whose research was aimed at achieving greater efficiency for certain human actions, in other words, their economic utilization.[58] There is an amazing fundamental affinity between the methods of science and engineering, on the one hand, and the development of *De Stijl* art on the other – from the schematic depiction of actual objects through stylized figures to the mathematically and technically constructed abstract depiction of objects.

Piet Mondrian

Lozenge with Colour Planes, 1919
Ruit met kleurvlakken
Oil on canvas, 49 x 49 cm
Rijksmuseum Kröller-Müller, Otterlo

*Mondrian originally painted this picture as a
traditional square composition in which the abstract pattern was entirely diagonal. Only later
did he turn the painting by 90°, so that it became
a diamond-shaped composition with vertical and
horizontal lines.*

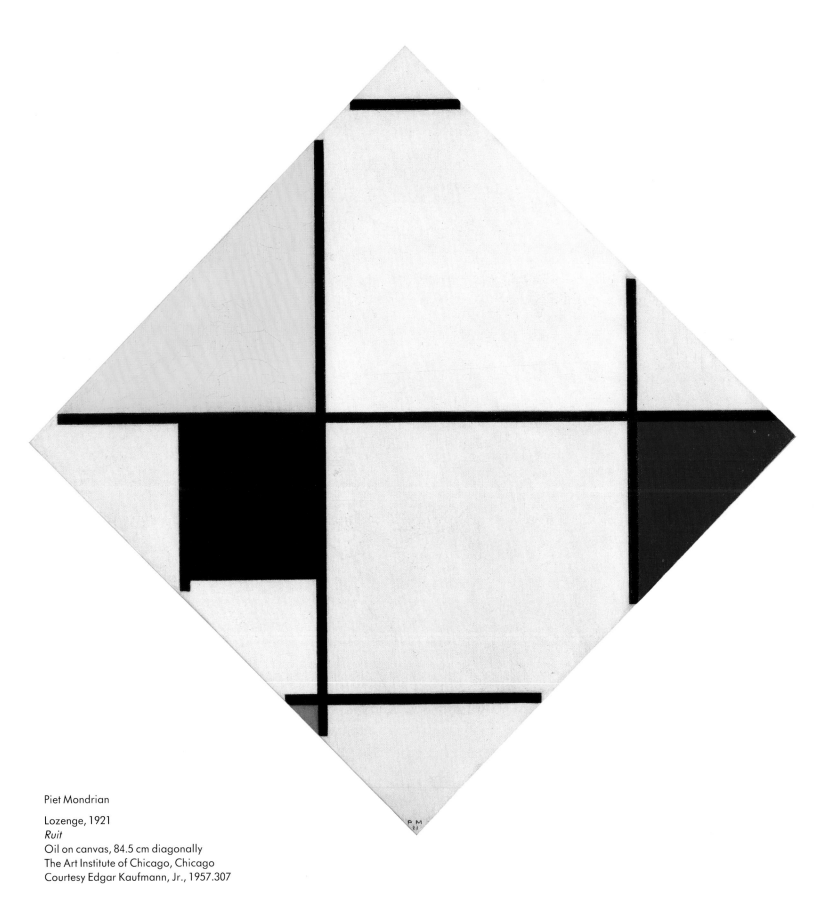

Piet Mondrian

Lozenge, 1921
Ruit
Oil on canvas, 84.5 cm diagonally
The Art Institute of Chicago, Chicago
Courtesy Edgar Kaufmann, Jr., 1957.307

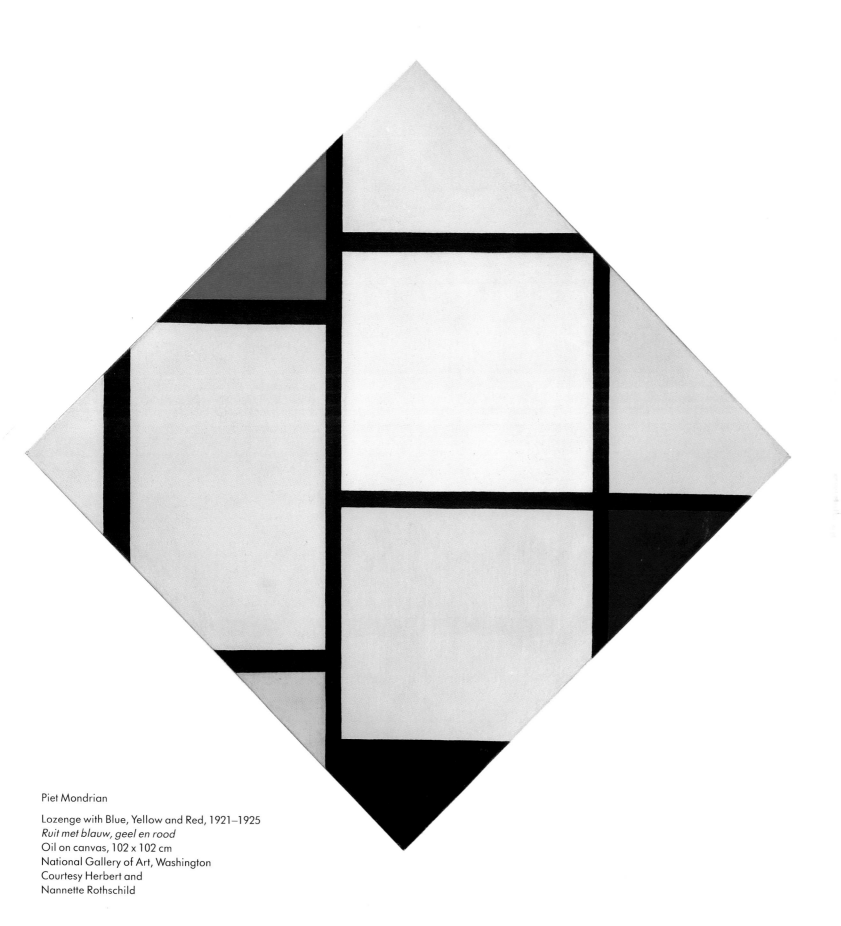

Piet Mondrian

Lozenge with Blue, Yellow and Red, 1921–1925
Ruit met blauw, geel en rood
Oil on canvas, 102 x 102 cm
National Gallery of Art, Washington
Courtesy Herbert and
Nannette Rothschild

Piet Mondrian

Lozenge with Blue, 1926
Ruit met blauw
Oil on canvas, 85 x 85 cm
A.E. Gallatin Collection,
Philadelphia Museum of Art

72

This totally rationalistic feature also explains why *De Stijl* artists did not follow other ways of achieving abstraction in art. Their discussion with Kandinsky shows that although they often found such approaches instructive, they nevertheless rejected them as unacceptable for "proper" art on the grounds that they were irrational and individualistic.[59]

This technoid approach to abstraction was connected with an ideological way of thinking that united a whole host of world views and philosophies, many of them traditional. The anthroposophical and, above all, theosophical ideals that moulded Mondrian and van Doesburg's minds mainly through the writings of Dr. M.H.J. Schoenmaeker were combined with the European tradition of philosophical idealism from Plato and Plotin to Hegel. In particular, we can trace the influence of the great 17th century Dutch philosopher Spinoza, especially his *Ethics*, on Mondrian and Vantongerloo.[60] Spinoza's mathematical and geometrizing method (of constructing his arguments "in a geometrical way") certainly left its mark, at least philosophically, on the mature stages of *De Stijl* art.

However, it should also be mentioned that the theoretical side of *De Stijl* did not keep up with these high standards. Its obvious syncretism is matched by an almost total lack of elementary techniques of correct philosophical argument. The quotations and concepts from a variety of sources were taken over without regard to their original context, even if the different views of the quoted scholars were totally incongruent. The central concepts of *De Stijl* theory – the Universal, the General, the Absolute, the Individual, Balance, Harmony, Dualism, Unity, Reality (also: Cosmic Reality), Purity, Zeitgeist, Evolution, etc. – were not defined, but simply taken for granted. As a result their content remained completely vague. Also, the line of argument in *De Stijl* led to circular conclusions: basic concepts were connected with other concepts in further stages of an argument, and the concepts with which they were linked were left undefined again, so that the circle of argument closed at the end of the chain, and the author's original assertion ended up as its own proof.[61]

Philosohically, *De Stijl* theory was irrelevant and far from original. This does not alter the fact that it yielded great works of art. After all, what matters in art is the quality of the results, not the quality of the intentions.

The critical point in the history of *De Stijl* was the rigid and almost relentless insistence on form with which their absolute aim was pursued. It meant that not only tradition had to be thrown overboard, but with it also many artistic inventions. As a result, there were quite a few differences of opinion and disaffections.

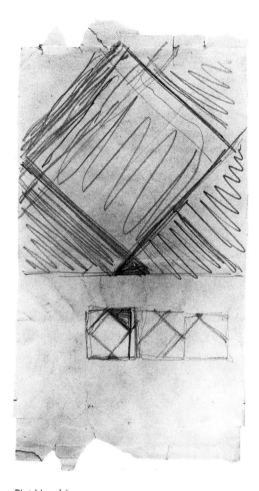

Piet Mondrian

Sketch for Four Lozenges, around 1925
Ontwerptekening voor vier ruiten
Pencil on paper, 27.3 x 14 cm
The Pace Gallery, New York

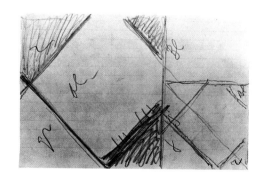

Piet Mondrian

Sketch for a Lozenge, 1925
Ontwerptekening voor een ruit
Pencil on writing paper, 16.8 x 24.1 cm
The Pace Gallery, New York

Robert van 't Hoff

Banister post as a sculpture for interior design
Trappaal ruimte-plastische binnenarchitectuur
Dimensions and location unknown

Van der Leck, for example, who did not wish to be restricted in his manner of expression, left *De Stijl* in March 1918, only six months after it had been founded.[62] Absolute abstraction had never been his aim, and all his paintings are therefore only abstract at first sight. They were abstract renderings and therefore always related to the visible reality of genuine natural phenomena. His paintings were the result of schematic abstraction and – unlike the mature works of Mondrian, van Doesburg, Domela and Vordemberge-Gildewart – not constructions of pure elements of colour and form. This is reflected in Bart van der Leck's paintings. The natural form of an individual object was often simply painted over and thus turned into a geometrical grid pattern, yielding a painting that appeared to be completely abstract.

Other artists with an undogmatic approach produced contradictions in their work. Vilmos Huszár, for example, who had made an important contribution to the breakthrough of a specifically abstract mode of expression in *De Stijl*, still completed a painting as late as 1928 whose vocabulary of form harked back to Theo van Doesburg's *Card Players* of 1916/17 (p. 45), combined with a scheme of prismatic penetration. This was his *Baccarat Players* (p. 86).

De Stijl is therefore far from unified. This was due not only to different views, but also to the exigencies of their utopian objectives, which gave importance to operating mechanisms from the very beginning. It was expressed programmatically in the editorial article (written by Theo van Doesburg) of the first issue of *De Stijl*: "It is the intention of this little magazine to make a contribution to the development of a new aesthetic awareness... As the public is not yet capable of experiencing this new plastic beauty, it will be the task of the expert to awaken a sense of beauty in the layman. A truly modern, i.e. conscientious, artist has a double calling: firstly to create a pure visual work of art, and secondly to make the public receptive to the beauty of purely visual art ..."[63]

This intention was bound to have its effect on the works of art themselves. Mondrian, for example, demanded right from the beginning that the artist should restrict his painterly expression to the three primary colours, that is, those colours which cannot be gained as a result of mixing others and therefore cannot be reduced in any way. These are red, blue and yellow. It did not mean, however, that Mondrian's paintings were therefore restricted to primaries from the moment *De Stijl* was founded. Although our inner eye always sees a world of images in which primary colours are related to each other in a complex system of relationships, the paintings which are generally regarded as typical of Mondrian and match this view are restricted to a certain period in his life – the 1920s. And even they are not unified. Most paintings of those years are simply referred to as *Composition with Red, Yellow and Blue* (e.g. pp. 23 and 62), though this brief title says very little about the true character of each picture.

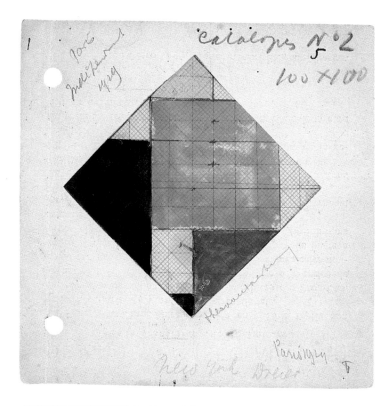

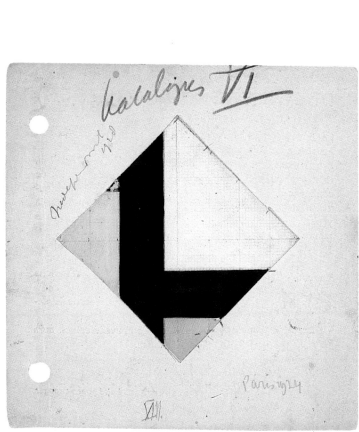

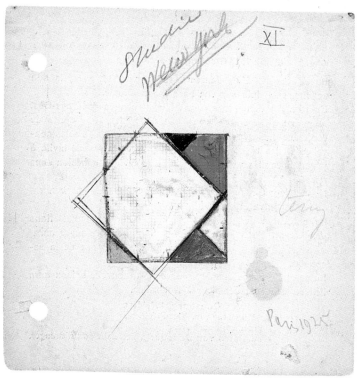

Theo van Doesburg

Sketches in a sketchbook, c. 1927
Schetsen in een schetsboek
Pencil and gouache on cardboard
Rijksdienst Beeldende Kunst, The Hague

These small studies come from a tiny book in which Theo van Doesburg made sketches of his own finished works. The collection was obviously intended as a works catalogue. Cf. also the illustrations of the original paintings on pp. 18, 58 and 77. The series is interesting because it shows van Doesburg's use of a grid pattern in his work.

Meudon, interior of Theo van Doesburg's studio and house. Photograph taken in the early Thirties.

We can see the artist's studio and, separated by wall partitions, his library and music room. On the walls are his Card Players *of 1916/17 and* Counter-Composition VIII *of 1924. Nowadays this painting is usually turned by 90°.*

Rather, it is characterized by the use of blue in several different refractions or with admixtures of white. Planes of this kind are obviously tints, i.e. something that was not supposed to occur in an ideal Neo-Plasticist painting. Theo van Doesburg therefore criticized Mondrian's tonal compositions,[64] referring to the abundant use of tonal shades in traditional works and, above all, in Impressionism, a style of avant-garde painting that was no longer modern. Doesburg saw tonal values as expressions of the painter's feelings; they were sentimental and therefore in disagreement with his rational view of art.

With their almost rigid orientation towards tonality, Mondrian's paintings of 1918 and 1919 seemed to be direct contradictions of his theoretical postulates. His diamond-shaped paintings, for example, are not composed of yellow, red and blue, but beige, ochre, grey-blue, pink, grey-brown, etc. If a viewer has certain preconceptions about Mondrian's art, he will therefore be even more surprised at the artist's *Composition with Red, Blue and Yellow-Green* (p. 67) of 1920. Here the most prominent colour is yellow-green – a secondary colour which is gained by mixing yellow and blue! This is all the more surprising when we consider that Mondrian found green totally unbearable – so much, in fact, that he would paint the leaf of an artificial tulip in his studio white.[65] Indeed this is not the only painting of that period with green in it![66] The other *De Stijl* artists also used green (pp. 27, 48 and 66). It seems no more logical or consistent than the constructions of relationships between colour and form, with shades of red, blue and yellow as well as black, white and shades of grey. After all, grey is not really a primary colour at all, but the result of mixing black and white.

These confusing manifestations can be explained by the desired effect and indeed the didactic intention of *De Stijl* art. Mondrian, Huszár and van Doesburg were trying to master in practice what they had conceived in theory: the concrete rendering of the absolute. And in doing so they wanted to be understood by others. Van Doesburg once said to Mondrian that not many people at that time had reached a stage in their development where they could understand the form-like character of colour. It was therefore necessary to use shades of colour that were closer to nature than pure primaries: "I change pure colours in the direction of black, white or grey for this current age, adapted to current surroundings and the world outside. It does not mean that I would not prefer pure colours."[67]

Apart from their didactic intention which took account of historically conditioned response mechanisms, the *De Stijl* artists were also faced with the fundamental difficulty of creatively putting an absolute postulate into practice. They wanted to show harmony in a great variety of case studies, harmony as a synthesis of balanced opposites and something that overcomes the incompatible. This necessarily meant that they were constantly trying to find different solutions to a problem that remained equally difficult. The ornamental principle, mechanisms of stylization, geometrical forms, the use of primary colours, colourless planes and lines – none of these elements could ever do more than point

towards the solution. The solution itself had to be found again and again. The genesis and history of *De Stijl* paintings illustrate this point.

Mondrian's treatment of colour, drawing and composition techniques as well as picture formats was a case in point. His preliminary sketches are always documents of a hard search. He started a composition by simply drawing and defining a shape, trying out different ways, drawing lines, erasing them again, shifting and redefining them and examining their value in relation to the whole (p. 62). The final composition then showed how these tentative experiments gradually yielded a certain distribution of planes and how colour was only added later as a second basic element, so that the definition of planes as a system of lines had to be re-examined (p. 63).

In the course of this search for ideal form Mondrian not only continually redefined lines and colours, but he also worked on the re-examination and further development of elementary techniques of depiction. His famous monochrome diamond-shaped composition of 1918, which consisted entirely of white and grey, is characterized by a concatenation of vertical, horizontal and oblique lines so that it is a combination of rectangles and equilateral triangles. What is more, the painting technique actually turned into the depicted content itself, i.e. the way in which the area of the painting was divided so as to yield a grid pattern. The two so-called *Draughts Board* paintings (pp. 24 and 25) and the diamond-shaped compositions of 1919 (p. 65) were

Theo van Doesburg

Counter-Composition of Dissonances XVI, 1925
Contra-compositie van dissonanten XVI
Oil on canvas, 100 x 180 cm
Gemeentemuseum, The Hague

Theo van Doesburg

Simultaneous Counter-Composition, 1929
Simultane contra-compositie
Oil on canvas, 50 x 50 cm
The Museum of Modern Art, New York

achieved in the same way, and Mondrian was not the only *De Stijl* painter who used this method. Theo van Doesburg did the same (p. 10), and so did Huszár, whose painting *Hammer and Saw* (p. 87) was also based on a grid pattern.[68]

The first *De Stijl* discussion on the use of oblique lines – always seen with a view to spatial effects – was triggered off by Bart van der Leck in 1918. He had used diagonals on the same footing as verticals and horizontals. Van Doesburg refused to accept such forms because the exclusively dynamic character of oblique lines introduced the element of perspective into the composition and thus an illusion of space which had to be overcome. Mondrian, on the other hand, accepted the suggestion and re-examined his methods in this light. Until then he had always placed his right angles parallel to the edges of the painting. In 1919 he followed van der Leck's example and painted a picture in which rectangular planes were set diagonally against the edges. The work still exists but is always shown differently from the way it was created by the artist at the time (p. 68). This is because Mondrian was not satisfied with the obvious way in which the diagonal was made absolute, and we know from one of his letters to van Doesburg that he decided spontane-

Georges Vantongerloo

Group $y = -ax^2 + bx + c$
$y' = -2ax + b$
$y = \dfrac{-ax^2 + bx + c}{-2ax + b}$
Red, Yellow, Green 1931
Groupe $y = -ax^2 + bx + c$
$y' = -2ax + b$
$y = \dfrac{-ax^2 + bx + c}{-2ax + b}$
Rouge, jaune, vert
Oil on canvas, 129 x 114 cm
Private collection

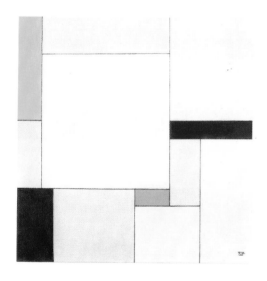

Georges Vantongerloo

Composition in a Square, Yellow, Green, Blue
and Indigo Orange, 1930
Composition en carré, jaune, vert, bleu, indigo-orange
Oil on canvas, 55 x 55 cm
Private collection, Zurich

ously to tilt the square composition and hang it up diagonally so that it became a lozenge. And the diagonal lines automatically became vertical and horizontal! The idea may also have been prompted by outward circumstances, when Mondrian had to send in new paintings to an art exhibition in February 1919. While the painting still had diagonals, he did not find it convincing – and so he simply tilted it a bit. This may also explain why Mondrian did not want to exhibit the two diamond-shaped paintings that had oblique lines whichever way they were looked at (pp. 61 and 65).[69]

This inspiration of a moment subsequently became one of Mondrian's special and indeed typical compositional features. He even had an easel made without a crossbar, so that the technical basis of his tools would not force him to paint diagonals as such.[70] So Mondrian's attitude towards diagonals was subject to a dialectical development whereby they were first regarded as positive reference points in his compositional thinking and finally negative ones, which they remained until the end. Although he later painted all his famous primary colour lozenges (p. 177) with the new easel, they were originally conceived as systems of diagonal lines.

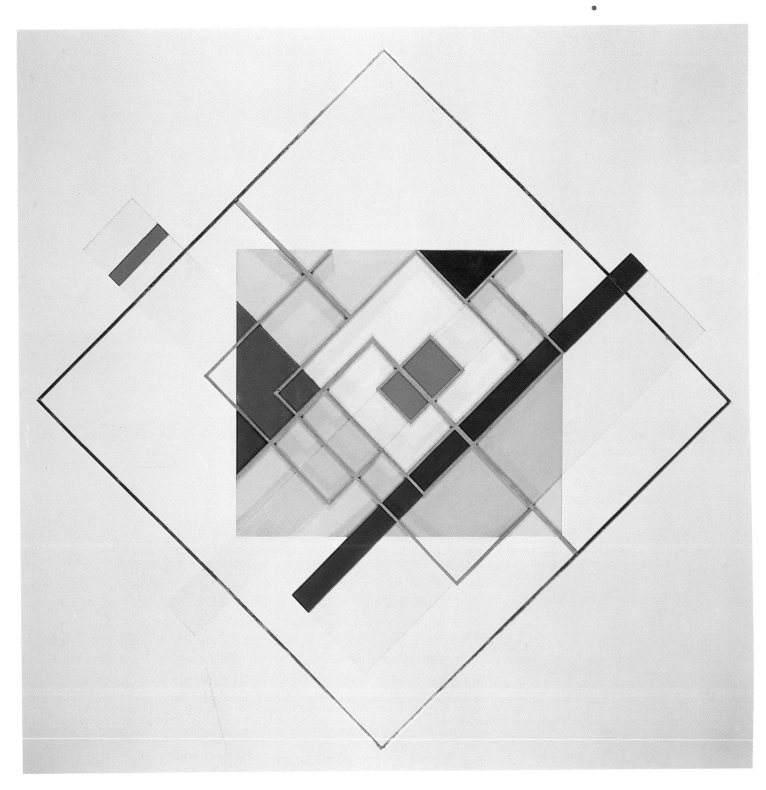

César Domela

Neo-Plastic Composition No. 10, 1930
Composition néo-plastique No. 10
Wood, copper and plexiglass,
110 cm diagonally
Gemeentemuseum, The Hague

This can be gathered from statements by the artist himself, because a number of preliminary sketches from the mid-Twenties have survived in which he planned diamond-shaped paintings as diagonal compositions on the rectangular surface of sketch paper (p. 73).[71] Interestingly, van Doesburg's view was diametrically opposed to Mondrian's on this point. Van Doesburg changed his ideas in the mid-Twenties when his theory developed into a conviction he called Elementarism. He regarded it as a consistent development of the *De Stijl* ideals of autonomous art. It was marked by the explicit reintroduction of oblique lines, a move that was to incorporate the inherent principle of dynamics. Van Doesburg put it this way: "The rectangular composition in which extreme tensions, horizontals and verticals had been neutralized was a relic from the classical tradition, and therefore displayed a certain homogeneity with the static state of architecture. The counter-composition (or anti-static composition) has liberated itself from this uniformity. Its diametrically opposed relationship with architecture (though on a different level) can be compared to the contrast between flat, white architecture and grey nature with all its curves. Elementarism has now liberated painting completely from conventions."[72]

Mondrian saw this quite differently: "Mondrian may have kept the rectangular relationship of vertical and horizontal lines, but he turned them by 45 degrees. This was done in opposition to the natural aspect of reality. He called his concept 'Elementarism'. In this way he put the emphasis on the means of expression, whereas I assigned the same significance to the relationship between them as to those methods."[73] What was regarded as progress by van Doesburg was considered to be a step back by Mondrian. This shows more than a difference in views on the correct use of artistic means: it was a controversy about the meaning of art. Once Mondrian had found his theories, he did not change them, but merely varied them.

Van Doesburg, on the other hand, believed that art had to be continually redefined and its means of expression changed again and again precisely because of its orientation towards the absolute. So what Mondrian regarded as linear progress towards the best possible result in the implementation of unchanging ideas was seen by van Doesburg as a new development and the continuous adaption to social progress. He commented in a letter to Anthony Kok: "As I was unable to imagine that the composition of equal relationships should be the final result of spiritual painting, I arrived at counter-compositions in 1924. I presented these findings in my manifestoes on Elementarism (*De Stijl* Nos. 73–76). And so I went from composition to construction, whereas now, in 1929, I have broken with all arrangements or compositions that are carried by emotions... It is the controllable form which I claim for painting, sculptures and architecture."[74]

Georges Vantongerloo

Construction in a Sphere, 1917/18
Construction dans la sphère
Mahogany, painted yellow, 17 cm diameter
Vantongerloo Heritage Collection

Van Doesburg's continually new approaches can be traced in his paintings: his early works consisted largely of square planes with linear structures. These were followed by paintings that were often totally devoid of border lines, but had colour planes directly adjacent to one another. Finally he painted simultaneous counter-compositions in

Georges Vantongerloo

Composition from an Oval, 1918
Composition émanante de l'ovoíde
Mahogony, painted blue, yellow and red,
16.5 x 6.5 x 6.5 cm
Private collection

which linear structures and different configurations of colour planes overlapped each other. Van Doesburg also changed his paintings by hanging them up in different ways so that new effects were achieved by simply turning them one way or the other. Photographs of his house in Meudon (p. 76) show that his black and white *Counter-Composition VIII* (p. 18) of 1924 was sometimes on his wall as a lozenge and sometimes as a square. He did the same with his *Counter-Composition V* of 1924 (p. 58).[75]

The use of art for utopian objectives meant that mathematical forms of language became important for *De Stijl*. "In the same way," wrote Vantongerloo, "that mathematics is the most obvious way of understanding things objectively, art is the most suitable way of feeling aesthetically."[76] The correspondence between mathematics and objective truth led *De Stijl* artists to adopt geometry as a stylistic method to express objectivity and to see mathematics as the equivalent of art.[77]

Georges Vantongerloo took these principles to radical extremes. His paintings must be understood as artistic implementations of dimensional relations which could also be expressed in the pure language of mathematics. Many of his paintings therefore do not have traditional titles, but mathematical equations. Where mathematics has formulae,

Georges Vantongerloo

$3\sqrt{L}=h$ $4\sqrt{L}=b$ $5\sqrt{L}=L$
geometrical Place, 1931
$3\sqrt{L}=h$ $4\sqrt{L}=b$ $5\sqrt{L}=L$
lieu géométrique
Grey wood, 46.5 x 55 x 38 cm
Private collection

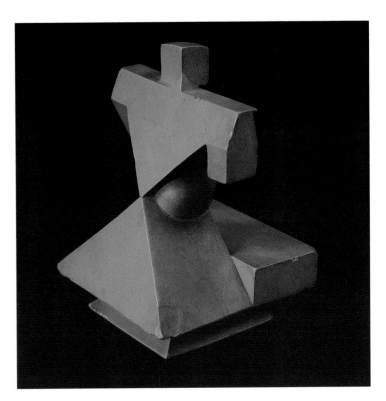

Georges Vantongerloo

Construction in a Sphere, 1918
Construction dans la sphère
Wood, painted blue, 18 x 12 x 12 cm
Private collection

the painter uses forms consisting of different planes with different colours. The harmonization of relations is common to all *De Stijl* artists, but, unlike the others, Vantongerloo did not want to have his expressiveness restricted by a gulf between art and the powerful and comprehensive language of mathematics. (This is why he turned away from *De Stijl* in 1922.)[78] And so he did not confine himself to rectangles, but also studied the potential of other ideal basic geometrical figures, such as the circle, the oval and the sphere. He also refused to be restricted to the three primary colours, even for the sake of consistent abstraction. Unlike Mondrian, who was a dogmatist, he based his work on the shape of a disc because its rotation could bring forth an ideal mixture of colours.[79] His greater scope of expressive means was matched by his creative diversity. Vantongerloo was not only a painter, but also a sculptor, the only sculptor among *De Stijl* artists.

His sculptures all follow a geometrical method of construction, with ideal shapes such as spheres and squares. Following van Doesburg's idea, Vantongerloo also studied the abstract renderings of objects by other avant-garde sculptors, though he was not satisfied with their intuitive method, for example Archipenko's – an approach that he felt was the exact opposite of his rational, mathematical mind.[80] Vantongerloo's sculptures, too, are modelled on nature. Like other *De Stijl* artists, however, he used the idea of reducing forms by schematizing them. He did this by reducing a given image to a configuration of several ideal planar and plastic geometrical shapes which he then turned into a sculpture. His *Construction in a Sphere*, which was based on a sketch of a seated women, illustrates this point (above and page right).[81]

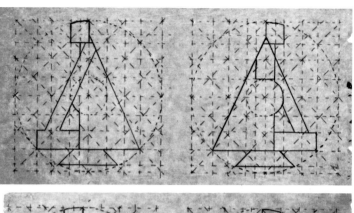

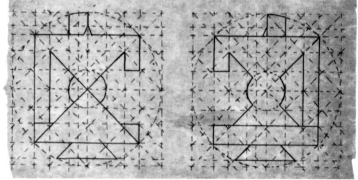

Vantongerloo also experimented with a combination of colour and three-dimensional form in his sculptures. He would transfer his primary colours onto the sculpture and then achieve different forms of unity between a planar and spatial effect.[82] It was only in the later stages of *De Stijl* that sculpting came to the fore again in Domela's object paintings.[83] These paintings combine, as it were, the artistic methods of Mondrian and van Doesburg and include the third dimension through the use of different materials. Though with differences in emphasis, he used glass, tin, wood, etc. to achieve a multifaceted synthesis of planar and plastic art (p. 80).

In this way different approaches to the creative possibilities of abstraction generated different vocabularies of form in the history of *De Stijl*. On the whole, *De Stijl* art displays an oddly paradoxical picture. The reason is that the complex structure of their vague utopian idea only permitted a one-sided link with reality. This can be seen in *De Stijl*'s attitude towards the earth-shaking political developments and revolutions of the time. *De Stijl* artists were convinced that bourgeois society with its individualism would be replaced by a mass society, and so they generally welcomed the Russian Revolution. But, with the exception of Robert van 't Hoff, they totally rejected any direct political role of art and any agitation in the service of Socialist or Communist propaganda.

Georges Vantongerloo

Four studies for *"Construction in a Sphere"*, 1918
4 études pour "construction dans la sphère"
Pencil on transparent paper
Vantongerloo Bequest

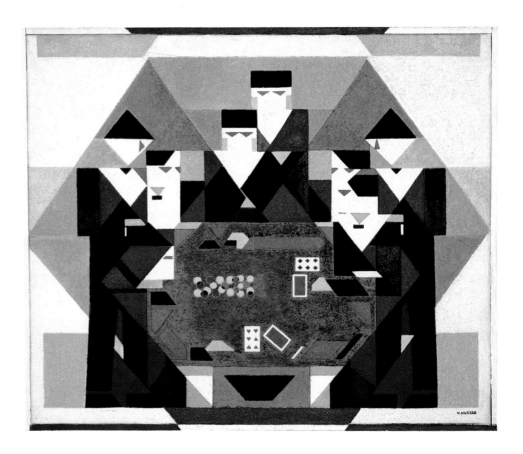

Vilmos Huszár

Baccarat Players, 1928
Baccaratspelers
Oil on canvas, 67.6 x 82.2 cm
Thyssen-Bornemisza Collection, Lugano

Many of them supported a petition in 1919 against the severance of postal links with the new Soviet Union, a policy that had been arbitrarily proclaimed by the Dutch government,[84] even though van Doesburg categorically opposed the subordination of art to Communist ideology, as demanded by Communist artists, on the grounds that it completely contradicted the basic idea of the liberation of the arts.

His creed was, "Art, as we demand it, is neither proletarian nor bourgeois. It is strong enough to influence the whole of art."[85] And: "There is no such thing as art created by a proletarian, because a proletarian ceases to be a proletarian as soon as he creates a work of art. He becomes an artist. An artist, however, is neither a proletarian nor a bourgeois. He belongs to everyone. Art is a mental skill in a person, aimed at liberating him from life's chaos and tragedy. Art is free to choose its own means; it is only bound by its own laws and nothing else. As soon as a work becomes a work of art, it transcends all differences between social classes."[86] For van Doesburg the freedom of art was therefore the most important basis of all thought and action. This explains why, throughout his life, he felt that Dadaism was the most consistent form of art and the core concept of his existence as an artist. He even regarded himself as a Dadaist, signed letters as "Dada-Does" and addressed Mondrian as "Dada-Piet".[87]

De Stijl artists kept out of politics and political theories, an attitude that was in keeping with their view of art as something greater than political or social reality. There was no other basis on which they could believe that abstract art was the only form of art appropriate to utopian ideals. In their idealism they were not concerned with social reality or economic structures, because they saw these as opposed to the free power of the human spirit, a force that was sufficiently powerful in itself to dissolve social antagonisms through the exemplary nature of a work of art and its effect on society. This also explains why the development of De Stijl was accompanied at a very early stage by the artists' involvement in the various genres of applied art.

Vilmos Huszár

Still Life Composition "Hammer and Saw", 1917
Stillevencompositie "Hammer en zaag"
Oil on wood, 31.5 x 53.5 cm
Gemeentemuseum, The Hague

Gerrit Rietveld

Rietveld-Schröder House, Utrecht 1924
Upper floor, reconstructed in 1987

5: Ideals in Practice

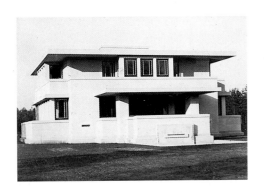

Robert van 't Hoff

Villa Henny, Huis ter Heide, 1914–1919
View while under construction
*The pond outside the terrace has not been
built yet.*

The artistic ideals of *De Stijl* spanned such a broad spectrum that the movement affected virtually every sphere of life, down to the smallest detail. *De Stijl* artists worked as architects, interior designers, furniture designers, commercial artists, etc., and their art was correspondingly diversified, thus showing their discrepancy between utopian ideas and reality. After all, their ideals and therefore also their projects could only be realized within a practical framework.

The topic of architecture already came up in the first issue of *De Stijl*, when Oud presented plans for a seaside promenade. These plans never came to anything.[88] The most important starting point and example for *De Stijl* architecture was the work of the American Frank Lloyd Wright.[89] One of his buildings, the *Villa Robie* in Chicago, was shown as early as the fourth issue of the magazine, with a photograph, a ground plan and an analysis by Oud. This was hardly surprising when we consider that Wright's vocabulary of form had already influenced a building in the Netherlands, *Villa Henny*, which was subsequently emulated by *De Stijl* architects. Robert van 't Hoff, who had met Wright in America, had been working on this building in Huis ter Heide near Zeist since 1914.[90]

The analysis of *Villa Henny* enabled Vilmos Huszár to put these new architectonic principles into words.[91] He judged the building by its compositional elements, i.e. from the point of view of the architect (walls, windows and functionality), the painter (colours, lines and planar forms) and the sculptor (plasticity and space). He then deduced some basic criteria for the selection of materials. To match the intellectual and rational basis of this new art, natural materials were no longer considered suitable, and Huszár suggested reinforced concrete instead, because it was artificial. This shows the application of the basic ideas of utopian art as developed in painting.

Architecturally, van 't Hoff's building was certainly a historical landmark. It was one of the first European examples of a building based on reinforced concrete boards and pillars, so that it became known as *Betonvilla* ("Concrete Villa") or *Betonhuis* ("Concrete House").

Situated in the country, *Villa Henny* is a very spacious building with two floors of over 2,000 square feet (about 200 square metres) each. It was modelled on Wright's so-called *Prairie Houses,* which served as examples for building inexpensive residential houses with an extremely simplified vocabulary of form.[92] Van 't Hoff used Wright's ideas for a scheme in which he created harmony between the basic elements of two-dimensional planes, plasticity and space. The architectonic design anticipated the decomposition of the closed volume into various configurations of colour planes, which later became the central theme of *De Stijl* architecture. This was achieved partly by choosing grey as the colour of the stringcourses between the floors, so that they stood out against a system of horizontal and vertical white planes, partly by placing the supports slightly further back, so that they seemed like margin decorations leaning against the walls, and finally by using a series of red and brown front windows.[93]

The most outstanding characteristic is the interdependence of different forms. The structure of the exterior is matched inside the building by the use of lines as a formative element, thus anticipating later *De Stijl* projects. This interdependence unfolds in a cohesive system of forms counteracting one another. The basic shape of the house is a square. A varied overall appearance is achieved by attaching various elements – i.e. terraces and window boxes – to the two floors or by reducing space in the form of retracted corners. It also affects the distribution of the rooms which differs on the two floors. The ground floor, which is closed and blocky, is only enlivened by a terrace and by retracted corners. This is matched by the division of the rooms into two functional groups: the extremely large lounge and dining room stretches along the whole front and has several small sitting rooms and studies attached to it at the back. The rooms are interspersed by some purely functional rooms, such as a kitchen, a bathroom and a toilet. The top floor is arranged quite differently: it is cross-shaped and based on a square. The distribution of bedrooms, guest rooms and children's playrooms takes this into account, forming a system where each room matches another.

The principle of additions and juxtapositions of square and long rectangular shapes follows a symmetrical arrangement on both floors, though this is broken and therefore varied by individual details. While the upstairs rooms are square, the ones on the ground floor are mainly long rectangles, so that the interdependence of forms is a matter of opposites. Outside, the same is true for the two side walls, which also match one another, while the front and back differ. Seen from outside, the ceiling between the two floors and the roof of the house also serve as conspicuous structural elements. They form the basis of an ingenious lighting system. The large canopy above the terrace outside the lounge and dining room provides shade for the large glass window, with light reflected from the pond in front of the canopy to the inside of the house. Upstairs the staircase, the bathroom and the washbasins in the bedrooms are illuminated by skylights. To avoid the use of sound insulation between the rooms, van 't Hoff inserted several small rooms for various functional and domestic purposes between them.

The most impressive feature of the house is its consistent lack of any decorative elements whatever as well as its consistent use of planes, lines and space, so that the building can also be understood as a large sculpture. This is reflected in the view, stated by Bart van der Leck, that architecture should be seen as the most principled type of sculpture.[94]

Another early *De Stijl* project, undertaken by members of the group before the founding of the magazine, was the *Villa Allegonda* in Katwijk aan Zee, started in 1916.[95] Oud was commissioned to redecorate an existing house, which he did together with Menso Kammerlingh Onnes and Theo van Doesburg. Oud and Kammerlingh Onnes, who was very much under the influence of North African architecture, turned this house on the beach into an asymmetrical group of cubically arranged blocks – the first example of asymmetrical yet strict forms with a free floor plan.

Menso Kamerlingh Onnes (design)
and Jacobus Johannes Pieter Oud (architecture)

Villa Allegonda, Katwijk aan Zee, 1916–1917
View of side facing away from the sea

Jacobus Johannes Pieter Oud

Villa Allegonda, Katwijk aan Zee
after renovation, 1927
View of side facing the sea

Robert van 't Hoff

Villa Henny, Huis ter Heide, 1914–1919
Exterior view

The building is highly ambivalent and full of tension. Its combination of open versus closed planes, protruding versus recessed ones and illuminated versus shady parts make the house seem like a large sculpture. This combination of opposites is a consistent design principle. Based on a square floor plan, designed and started before the founding of De Stijl, it displays a degree of symmetrical structure that runs counter to the ideals of De Stijl. But the dialetical interdependence of mutually contradicting forms anticipates an important element of typical De Stijl design. The internal structure is ingeniously reflected in the exterior view. The ground floor and the top floor are divided up completely differently. While the ground floor has two large areas (a long rectangular lounge and various functional rooms) facing one another, the top floor is based on the shape of a cross, with the various rooms arranged accordingly. The same opposites are reflected in the side views of the house. A continuous stretch of eight windows on the ground floor is matched by four windows in the centre, flanked by clearly recessed walls. Thus we can easily discern the cross-shaped arrangements of the rooms on the top floor, especially when viewed diagonally.

However, such outside/inside correspondences are deceptive. On the side of the garden a terrace with a canopy protrudes from the building. At the front of the villa the terrace is matched by a protruding entrance section. This suggests a continuous longitudinal axis which does not exist inside. With this building Robert van 't Hoff merged two totally different architectonic principles: the architectural villa tradition going back to Palladio and Frank Lloyd Wright's Prairie Houses.

Villa Henny, Huis ter Heide, 1914–1919
View of the exterior, and floor plans of the
ground and top floors.

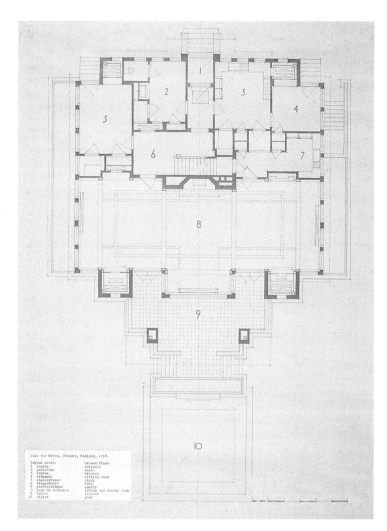

Huis ter Heide, Utrecht, Holland, 1916.

Begane grond.	Ground floor.
1 ingang	entrance
2 garderobe	coats
3 keuken	kitchen
4 zitkamer	sitting room
5 studeerkamer	study
6 trappenhuis	hall
7 provisiekamer	pantry
8 woon en eetkamer	living and dining room
9 terras	terrace
10 vijver	pond

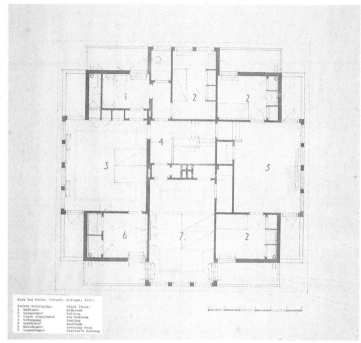

Huis ter Heide, Utrecht, Holland, 1916.

Eerste verdieping.	First floor.
1 badkamer	bathroom
2 slaapkamer	bedroom
3 eigen slaapkamer	own bedroom
4 bovengang	landing
5 werkkamer	workroom
6 kleedkamer	dressing room
7 logeerkamer	visitor's bedroom

Nearly half of the ground floor is occupied by the big south-facing lounge/dining room that looks out towards the garden. North of it, towards the entrance, is a functional section which includes a hall, a small corridor, a bathroom, a toilet and a kitchen. West of this central complex is a small study, and east of it a small sitting room with a fairly big utility room next to it, on its eastern side. Both from this room and from the hall there are doors leading to the big lounge and dining room. As in Frank Lloyd Wright's Prairie Houses, the centre of the house is a fireplace.

The arrangement of rooms on the top floor seems to be at an angle compared with the ground floor. Here are the two biggest rooms, the parents' bedroom, a study and children's playroom facing east and west, respectively. Adjoining them is a bathroom and a dressing room in the west, as well as a children's bedroom in the east. The arrangement is rounded off by another children's bedroom in the north and a guest room in the south.

95

Jacobus Johannes Pieter Oud

De Vonk holiday residence, Noordwijkerhout, 1917-1918
View of building while under construction

In 1927 *Villa Allegonda* was rebuilt by Oud and then later turned into a tourist hotel. Theo van Doesburg designed two glass windows for the building, *Composition II* of 1917 and *Composition V* of 1918 (p. 51). The former was put in the stairwell between the added turret and the renovated parts of the previous building. According to Oud himself, this totally abstract stained glass window, which is now lost, showed the rhythmically rising movements of a storm tide. The location of the second composition, of which we only have the draft, is not known.[96]

When van Doesburg and Oud built *De Vonk* (The Spark), their collaboration was similar, but more comprehensive. *De Vonk* was a holiday residence for female workers in Noordwijkerhout, about 6 miles (10 km) from Leiden, on the North Sea.[97] This time their client was not a wealthy businessman, but a welfare organization called *Leiden Volkshuis*, which was headed by the dedicated feminist Emilie Knappert. Oud was probably responding to the client's demands when he built a traditional three-storey house in the form of a long, rectangular object with wings; a house that was strictly symmetrical and had a saddleback roof with dormer windows. The ground floor was occupied by lecture rooms and a dining room; Emilie Knappert's flat had the central position of the first floor, and the workers' bedrooms were located on the second floor.

Theo van Doesburg designed tiled mosaics for the front of the building and the colourful decoration of the hallways, with abstract floor patterns and doors in two colours. These decorative elements were to counteract the conventional starkness of the building and the traditional limits of spatial effects and experience. Especially in the ground-floor stairwell this was the joint achievement of the painter and the architect. Here Oud created a cross-shaped hall with a staircase consisting of stepped blocks, arranged vertically and horizontally. Van Doesburg's floor mosaic, with yellow, black and white tiles, added an element of unrest to this sculpture-like structure. The same effect, though less prominent, can be noticed on the other floors, where it is reinforced by doors in different colours.

The founder of *De Stijl* participated in several similar projects at the time.[98] Among these, two villas and one hotel/restaurant, designed by Jan Wils, stand out in particular. Van Doesburg designed glass windows for the *De Lange* Villa in Alkmaar and *De Karperton* in Bergermeer.[99] His *Composition IV* (p. 49), a three-part ensemble at *De Lange*, occupies a window in the stairwell, also designed by van Doesburg. While this stairwell and window have been preserved, the five windows at the villa in Bergermeer have been lost. However, we still have four colour drafts titled *Small Pastoral Scenes*, whose totally abstract composition is said to be derived from rural motifs such as bulls and horses. The planes that were left white at the centre of each draft may have been intended to suggest the context of the motifs. Interestingly, van Doesburg also used secondary colours – green and brown – in this composition.

Jacobus Johannes Pieter Oud

De Vonk holiday residence, Noordwijkerhout
View of the building today

Jacobus Johannes Pieter Oud (architecture)
and Theo van Doesburg (walls and mosaic floor)

Entrance hall and stairwell at the *De Vonk*
holiday residence, Noordwijkerhout
View of the building in 1918

Theo van Doesburg

Colour design for the floor in the entrance hall,
the stairwell and the hallway on the ground floor
of the *De Vonk* holiday residence,
Noordwijkerhout, in 1918
*Kleurontwerp voor de tegelvloer in vacantiehuis
De Vonk, Noordwijkerhout*
Gouache and collage on grey cardboard,
98 x 73.5 cm
Rijksdienst Beeldende Kunst, The Hague

The floor pattern at the *De Vonk* holiday residence,
designed by van Doesburg: entrance hall with
stairwell and three further details of today's
building.

Theo van Doesburg

Colour draft for a glass mosaic at
Villa Allegonda, Katwijk aan Zee
Composition VI, 1917
*Kleurontwerp voor compositie VI
voor glasmozaiek*
Gouache, 74.4 x 31 cm
Private collection

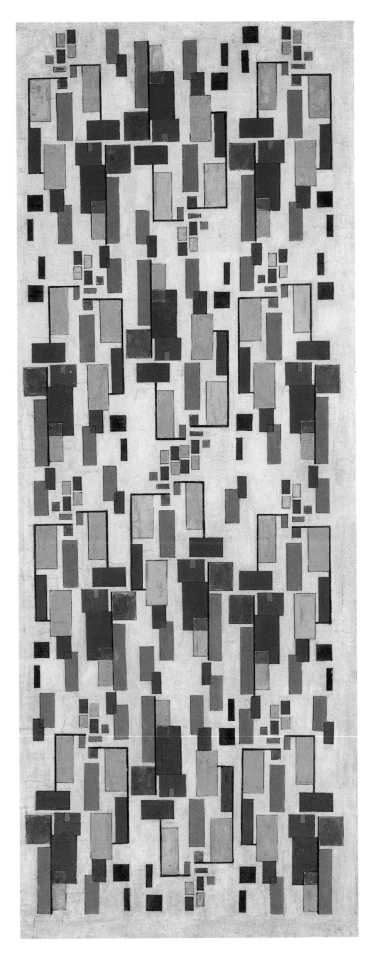

Jan Wils
De Dubbele Sleutel Hotel/Restaurant
Woerden, 1918
Exterior view

In 1918 Jan Wils and Theo van Doesburg worked together on another project, the rebuilding of the café and restaurant *De Dubbele Sleutel* (The Double Key) in Woerden, a town near Utrecht. Again, van Doesburg handled the colourful interior design, of which drafts have survived.[100] Jan Wils's architecture, however, was more important for *De Stijl*. Similarly to *Villa Allegonda*, designed by Oud, the architect was not free in his choice of form, because the size of the existing restaurant and the number of floors had to remain the same.[101] However, Wils was allowed to alter the floor plan for the distribution of rooms and to redesign the exterior. Like van 't Hoff's *Villa Henny*, this building was also noticeably influenced by Frank Lloyd Wright, though Wils varied the original idea far more freely, partly by emphasizing the expressive possibilities inherent in the use of different building materials. To some extent, therefore, the building also resembles Berlage's style under whom both Wils and Oud had studied architecture.

The most outstanding architectural and sculptural feature of the building is the dissolution of the architectonic substance in the form of numerous, mutually penetrating and supplementing blocks. Wils made consistent use of horizontal elements (stringcourses between floors, architraves, roof cornices, balustrades and frames for window boxes) as a way of uniting and unifying a building that was noticeably fragmented and vertically oriented. The dialectical interdependence of each supposedly independent element yields an extremely expressive ensemble, an impression which is further corroborated by the small planes of the brickwork and the smooth horizontal stringcourses. These two elements also accentuate the contrast between the two building materials that were used, brick and concrete. Thus antithesis and synthesis counteract each other and tension is created, so that the building, which was unfortunately demolished in the mid-Seventies, must have been very attractive indeed.

Jacobus Johannes Pieter Oud

Corner of Block VIII at the *Spangen* council
estate, Rotterdam 1919–1920
The Potgieterstraat façade, which was to be
designed in colour by Theo van Doesburg, is
continued on the right.

The hotel consists of autonomous blocks, i.e. components that are determined by the different functions of the various rooms inside. This explains why the whole building has so many different parts. Wils himself accurately described it as "externalization of the interior". In a critique in *De Stijl* Robert van 't Hoff described this principle as the advantage of rational architecture. At the same time, however, he felt that the use of brick was inadequate and that concrete would have yielded a much clearer plastic language.[102]

In 1918, the year when *De Dubbele Sleutel* was built, Oud became chief architect of the Rotterdam building authorities, and in the years to come he built a large number of apartment blocks.[103] In doing so, he kept within certain limits, which had a particularly negative effect on his early apartment blocks in the Spangen district of the city, where he was not permitted to carry out his own aesthetic ideas. Blocks I and V, designed in 1918 and completed in 1920, fell rather short of his first drafts. In particular, the use of hip roofs went against Oud's "affirmation of flat roofs and their consequences". The heavy blocks were packed too tightly together compared with the width of the street, so that they did not allow enough light to fall into the rooms. The floor plans, too, followed the conventions of the time. When Oud designed Blocks VIII and IX in 1919, he was allowed to use flat roofs, however. Also, the front of each block is structured in such a way that horizontal elements (bands of socles and roof edges) are counter-balanced by the dominating vertical elements of the window axes, so that the overall effect is a more interesting one. In particular, the design of the corners shows Oud's experiments in other areas. This is where he tried to implement inventions of *De Stijl* architecture. The stringcourses, which are arranged in a linear way, are continuous and also traverse the corners of the building. The balconies are recessed and therefore rectangular apertures between flat, vertical walls. Depending on the viewer's perspective, the walls appear either linear or planar and seem to be matched by the chimneys on the adjacent apartment blocks.[104]

Although the floor plans of the Spangen blocks followed a conventional pattern, they nevertheless reflected *De Stijl* concepts most closely. This is because Oud had worked on a model flat together with Theo van Doesburg and Gerrit Rietveld, who had recently joined *De Stijl*. It was given a firm structure by van Doesburg's colour scheme, while the furniture was designed by van Rietveld as a consistent implementation of his vocabulary of form, which he had attained in his *Red/Blue Chair*. His famous *Sideboard* (p. 126), for example, was an important part of the furniture, together with the *Red/Blue Chair* (p. 121). This flat was designed in 1919 and a sample was completed in 1920, but unfortunately we do not know whether it was really duplicated for all the other units – a step that would have been difficult to imagine in view of the widespread lack of understanding for this type of furniture.[105]

Theo van Doesburg

Colour draft for the façade of Block VIII,
Spangen, Rotterdam, 1921
*Kleurcompositie voor de gevel aan de
Potgieterstraat*
Ink and watercolour, 15.7 x 25.5 cm
Institut Néerlandais, Paris
Fondation Custodia

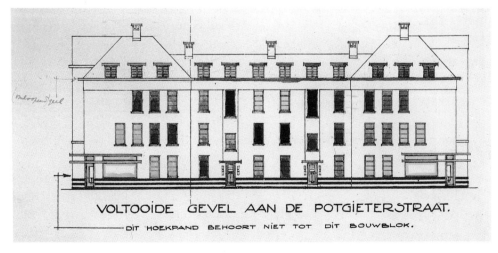

Theo van Doesburg

Colour draft for the façade of Block VIII,
Spangen, Rotterdam, 1921
*Kleurcompositie voor de gevel aan de
Potgieterstraat*
Ink and watercolour, 35.6 x 53.3 cm
Institut Néerlandais, Paris
Fondation Custodia

In 1921 Theo van Doesburg designed colour façades for Blocks VIII and IX in Spangen. The frames for the doors and windows were to be yellow, blue and green as well as black, grey and white. The arrangement of these strongly contrastive colours was explicitly intended to counteract the firmness of the heavy, solid brickwork so that the architectonic substance no longer appeared blocky and the shape of the building was not as conspicuous. Oud felt that this concept was mere aesthetic playfulness, and his argument with van Doesburg eventually led to his break with *De Stijl* in the autumn of 1921.[106]

However, during his time with *De Stijl*, Oud's own vocabulary of form was noticeably influenced by it, which can also be seen in the housing estates built after this period. *Oud-Mathenesse* formed part of Oud's 1923 plans for the extension of Rotterdam, but was originally conceived as a temporary project that was to last no longer than 25 years.[107] The limits within which he had to work were rather restrictive: the estate was small, in the shape of a narrow triangle and therefore not really suitable for this purpose, and Oud was expected to use steep saddle roofs. The estate included 343 units for families, eight shops and one administrative building. The houses were arranged symmetrically in several parallel streets around a central square where all the shops were situated. Each terraced house had a net living space of 595 square feet (55.3 square metres) and cost 2,050 guilders. It was made of semi-durable wood, painted white. This form, which was the result of certain exigencies, was to determine the direction of Oud's later housing projects.

Jacobus Johannes Pieter Oud

Project Manager's house
Built during the work on the *Oud-Mathenesse*
housing estate, Rotterdam, 1923

In 1924 Oud designed workers' houses as part of a larger housing estate at the Hook of Holland. Only two blocks were built (p. 106) in 1926/27, with a rounded corner pavilion at either end. Wall segments on the ground floor and lattices on the upper floor illustrate the measuring unit in an even rhythm of uniformly horizontal rows, with a single balcony extending from one end to the other. The programmatic features of this new art have all been implemented here: a flat roof, horizontal windows in light metal frames, plastered walls and large window panes. To enliven the overall effect, the architect also included multicoloured highlights. This had already been a feature of *Oud-Mathenesse*, with lines of yellow bricks, walls painted white, colourful doors and window frames and red roof tiles. Unlike his other projects, however, Oud arranged the bedrooms around the kitchen.[108]

The Hook of Holland plans were followed by plans for *Kiefhoek*, a housing estate south of Rotterdam, specially designed for large families (preliminarily designed in 1925 and built in 1928–1930, p. 106).[109] The authorities stipulated that the project should be as inexpensive as possible, at a time when the normal type would have cost 2,400 guilders. The terraced houses had three bedrooms upstairs and a sitting room, kitchen and toilet downstairs. Only 13 feet (4.1 metres) wide, they gave people a living space of 430 square feet (40 square metres). Oud's tight budget meant that the shower and washbasin on the upper floor as well as the hatch on the ground floor had to be omitted. He built the houses in such a way that the upper floor windows formed a continuous line, as did the plastered wall underneath.

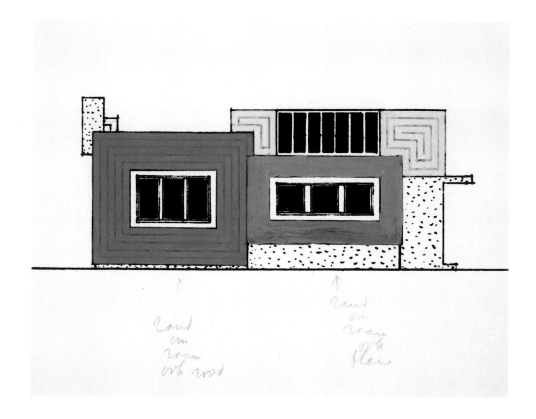

Jacobus Johannes Pieter Oud

Colour draft for the exterior of the Project Manager's house at *Oud-Mathenesse*, 1923
Kleurontwerp voor exterieur van de directiekeet in Oud-Mathenesse
Ink and watercolour
Nederlands Documentatiecentrum voor de Bouwkunst, Amsterdam

Jacobus Johannes Pieter Oud

Contemporary view of the housing estate at the
Hook of Holland, 1924–1927

Jacobus Johannes Pieter Oud

Contemporary view of the *Kiefhoek* housing
estate, Rotterdam, 1925–1930

The corners of the terraces were rounded off by semicircular balconies and round shop buildings. Unlike other estates, the individual units were separated by walls to prevent individual gardens from spoiling the overall effect. Again, the monotony of the terraces was relieved by yellow brickwork around the socle areas, grey sitting-room window frames, red doors against white walls and yellow window frames on the upper floor.

Due to the severe limitations imposed by the authorities, Oud could apply his new vocabulary of form only partly to these houses. But he was able to develop a more coherent design for the Project Manager's house of *Oud-Mathenesse* (pp. 104 and 105).[110] The building consisted of symmetrically interlocking cubes that seemed like autonomous elements, a principle which was further emphasized by the fact that each cube was in a different *De Stijl* colour. The rooms were arranged in the form of a cross around the cross-shaped hallway - a variation of Frank Lloyd Wright's method, which had already been emulated by Robert van 't Hoff in his *Villa Henny*. Windows only occurred on the sides, where they were arranged horizontally. There was a front door, matched only by a narrow slit at the back to let in the daylight. The simplicity of cubic architecture was counterbalanced by its decoration. Creating autonomous planar sections on all sides, an ingenious system of wooden panels playfully surrounded the basic form of the square in a number of different variations and in parallel horizontal and vertical arrangements with uniform pencilling. For example, the actual space was supplemented by a seemingly spatial, illusionary but nevertheless suggestive decor, so that the resulting irritation led to a planar balance of dimensions. This was an application of the central *De Stijl* idea of the harmonization of opposites. Although the building was demolished shortly afterwards, it was given international attention in architectural magazines, even contemporary ones.

In 1924 Oud used this decorative system of linear structuring for the façade of the *Café de Unie* on the Coolsingel in Rotterdam.[111] The café and restaurant was situated between two listed buildings (p. 109), and Oud wanted the façade of this house to break up the austere appearance of the street. It may have helped the consistent architectonic implementation of his idea that the *Café De Unie* was originally built to last no more than ten years (though it was only destroyed during the war, in 1940). The only axis element was the five-part window, arranged in a horizontal line, on the second floor. All other openings in the wall were situated on the sides. The composition was rounded off by two narrow plastic lines of text running downwards. The weighting of the façade was complemented by the colours, and a harmonious effect was achieved by the division of the large red plane into various sections.[112]

Café De Unie
Reconstructed at 25, Mauritsweg,
Rotterdam

Jacobus Johannes Pieter Oud

Colour draft for the façade of the *Café De Unie*,
Rotterdam, 1924, and vintage photograph of the
actual building on Coolsingel, completed in 1925
Nederlands Documentatiecentrum voor de
Bouwkunst, Amsterdam

*Together with the vintage photograph, the draft
gives an impression of the building which was
destroyed in 1940. In this draft Oud changed several details in the composition of the façade (the
red linear portions at the bottom have been omitted, and the windows there only have blue and
yellow frames).*

Theo van Doesburg

Colour draft for the exterior of terraced houses on *Torenstraat*, Drachten, 1921
Kleurontwerp voor het exterieur van de midden-standswoningen in de Torenstraatte, Drachten
Pencil, ink, watercolour and collage, 19 x 60 cm
Streekmuseum It Bleekerhûs, Drachten

Cees Rinks de Boer

Terraced houses on *Torenstraat*, Drachten, 1921

Oud used colours to complement the design of his buildings, though he distinguished them according to their different functions. "Free" buildings, such as the Rotterdam café and the Project Manager's House, were given a far more colourful exterior than the workers' houses. Theo van Doesburg's ideas were completely different. After he had been unable to realize his ideas on the Spangen apartment blocks while working with Oud, he managed to achieve his ambition in the little town of Drachten in Friesland.

Here, in 1921/22, van Doesburg designed comprehensive colour schemes for quite conventional brick buildings, built by the architect de Boer.[113] The artist designed some comprehensive plans for a number of middle-class houses on Torenstraat as well, the School of Agriculture on the other side and detached houses in various places. These plans

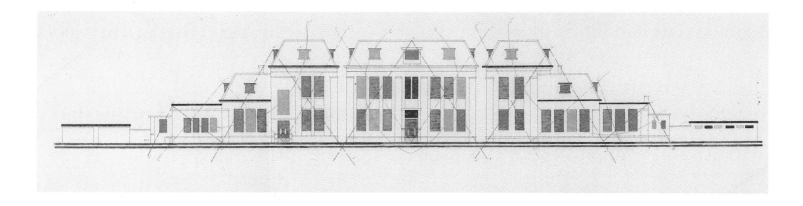

ranged from the colours for the façade through the interior to stained glass windows. In the same context he also designed the stained glass windows for his so-called *Great Pastoral Scene* (p. 55). For the Toren-straat buildings, a symmetrically arranged complex with two protruding corner buildings and a special emphasis on the central portion, van Doesburg developed a system of door and window frames which started from the centre and then rhythmically distributed primary colours in asymmetrical layers. This design of the façade visibly relieved the somewhat rigid and heavy appearance of the architecture. However, the inhabitants at that time, who referred to the housing estate rather sarcastically as *Papageienbuurt* (Parrot Estate), felt that the colours were too loud and soon painted over them.[114]

It was not until 1923 that Theo van Doesburg, in collaboration with the young architect Cornelis van Eesteren, succeeded in developing new concepts of this kind. His ambitious draft of a building for the University of Amsterdam never went beyond the planning stage – a large complex, arranged laterally in the shape of a cross and with extremely broad dimensions.[115] The project was van Eersteren's diploma thesis as a student of architecture. Again, van Doesburg contributed drafts for the colour design, including the walls, floors and ceiling, with a network of large, rectangular sections of primary colours. It culminated in the design of the ceiling for the Great Hall, where it took the form of a counter-composition (pp. 112/113). This ensemble would have achieved a far-reaching transcension of plastic design.

And so the years that followed the initial phase of *De Stijl* were full of experiments, intensive discussions and new developments as well as disaffections. Even before Oud turned his back on the movement, it was abandoned by Bart van der Leck, Jan Wils, Robert van 't Hoff and Vilmos Huszár. Nevertheless, all of them continued to be influenced for a long time by the vocabulary of form which they had developed together in the early years, so that later works, too, can also be regarded as belonging to the whole area of *De Stijl* design.[116]

Theo van Doesburg

Colour draft for the front and sides of the School of Agriculture in Drachten, 1921
Kleurontwerp voor de voor- en zijgevels van de Landbouwschool te Drachten
Pencil, ink and watercolour, 24.6 x 105.8 cm
Streekmuseum It Bleekerhûs, Drachten

In this draft van Doesburg folded the sides of the building to the front, thus emphasizing the continuous form of his colour scheme, which united both sides.

Theo van Doesburg

Colour draft for a university hall in Amsterdam,
1923
*Kleurontwerp voor de hal van een universiteit in
Amsterdam*
Pencil, gouache and collage, 63.4 x 146 cm
Nederlands Documentatiecentrum voor de
Bouwkunst, Amsterdam
Stichting van Eesteren-Fluck-Van Lohuizen

Jan Wils

Contemporary view of the completed buildings
for the housing estate of the *Daal en Berg*
cooperative society in Papaverhof,
The Hague, 1922

Jan Wils

Perspective draft for the housing estate of the
Daal en Berg cooperative society in Papaverhof,
The Hague, 1920
*Perspektieftekening voor de tuinstad "Daal en
Berg" in Papaverhof*
Ink on paper, 21.6 x 29.5 cm
Nederlands Documentatiecentrum voor de
Bouwkunst, Amsterdam

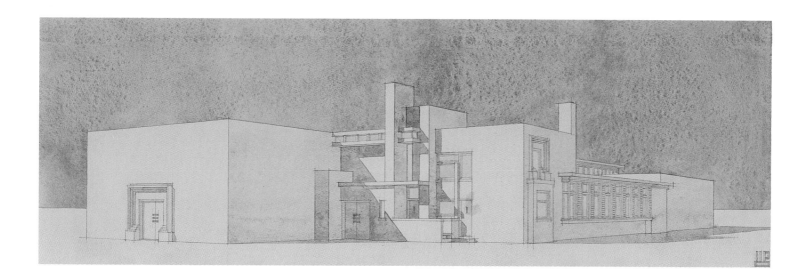

Jacobus Johannes Pieter Oud

Draft for a factory in Purmerend, 1919
Ontwerptekening voor een fabriek in Purmerend
Ink and watercolour
Nederlands Documentatiecentrum voor de
Bouwkunst, Amsterdam

Jans Wils, an architect whose attitude was largely pragmatic, made use of his *De Stijl* experience when he built the *Papaverhof* housing estate in The Hague for the *Daal en Berg* cooperative society from 1920 to 1922. This complex was to set an example for the typical housing estates of the Twenties and Thirties.[117] The architect arranged 128 middle-class houses around Papaverhof, a courtyard with grass and trees, 230 x 330 feet (70 x 100 metres). The nucleus was formed by 68 houses, arranged in a double ring. Two houses always formed a single unit, with a green patch shared between them and set at a slight angle to the next unit. They were built with sinter concrete, a material that was made with state-of-the-art technology at the time. This meant that the houses could be built more quickly and with better sound insulation. The two three-storey apartment blocks at either end with a total of 60 flats were built in the conventional way. The entire complex is a system of individual blocks set loosely at right angles, so that vertical and horizontal elements unite to form a rhythmically structured, lively whole. In this way it reflects the influence of *De Stijl* again, as well as Wright's vocabulary of form.

This broadening of *De Stijl* forms affected not only the building of residential houses. Relations with industry started at an early stage, and Oud made a name for himself with designs for a factory in Purmerend as early as 1919/20. He planned this factory as an ensemble of intersecting horizontals and verticals, structured asymmetrically.[118] This draft, which would have meant a far-reaching implementation of *De Stijl* ideals in architectonic design, was never put into practice.

In 1916 Vilmos Huszár had met the designer Piet Zwart and the architect Pieter Christophel Klaarhamer. In the next three years the three men worked on several different interior design projects. Their major client was Cornelis Bruynzeel Jr., who also owned the company of the same name. Partly still together with Jan Wils, at whose studio Piet Zwart was employed until 1921, they designed the furniture and interior decoration of Bruynzeel's private house *De Arendshoeve* in Voorburg.[119]

Vincent van Gogh

Van Gogh's Bedroom in Arles, 1889
Oil on canvas, 56.5 x 74 cm
Musée d'Orsay, Paris

Huszár took this famous painting by Vincent van Gogh as the starting point for his colour scheme of the boys' bedroom at De Arendshoeve, a villa in Voorburg. In two studies he produced a geometrized version of this composition, which then served as the basis of his own colour composition.

Apart from an advertising board for Bruynzeel, designed by Huszár as early as 1918, the interior design of *De Arendshoeve* yielded some important results. Klaarhamer and Zwart designed the furniture, and Huszár the overall colour scheme and the painting of the walls. This made it a self-contained ensemble, similar to the houses built by Oud, van Doesburg and Wils, who also used to collaborate on joint projects. While Klaarhamer and Zwart's were heterogeneous and only partly in line with *De Stijl* ideas, Huszár's colour design contributed to the creation of a spatial structure that was close to the objectives of *De Stijl*. However, the *Boys' Bedroom* was not published in *De Stijl* until 1922.[120] In 1919, when it was designed, van Doesburg and Zwart were at loggerheads with one another.[121] Also, the fact that Huszár published articles in the magazine *Levende Kunst* (Living Art), a competitor of *De Stijl* (with decidedly different ideals), made van Doesburg and Mondrian suspicious towards him, so that this period was marked by tension within the group.[122]

The *Boys' Bedroom* at *De Arendshoeve* (p. 117) was a major progressive achievement.[123] The interior no longer exists, but has been reconstructed by the Gemeentemuseum in The Hague according to old photographs. It consists of two beds, two chairs, a bedside table, washing facilities with two wash-basins and a chest-of-drawers for clothes.

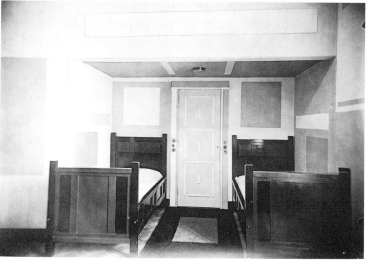

Vilmos Huszár (colour scheme)
and Pieter Jan Christophel Klaarhamer
(furniture)

Interior of the boys' bedroom in the Villa *De
Arendshoeve*, Voorburg, 1919
Reconstruction
Gemeentemuseum, The Hague

The furniture of this early De Stijl *interior is now
at the Gemeentemuseum in The Hague. Based on
vintage photographs, Huszár's drafts and with
the original furniture, it was possible to recon-
struct the room for the museum.*

Vintage photograph of the interior design of the
boys' room at the Villa *De Arendshoeve* in
Voorburg

Vilmos Huszár (colour design)
and Pieter Zwart (furniture)

Interior of the sitting room at the
Villa *De Arendshoeve*, Voorburg, 1921

*Vintage photograph, showing an obvious differ-
ence between the rather conventionial furniture
oriented towards the forms of the Viennese
Workshop and the typical* De Stijl *colour scheme
of the room. However, Piet Zwart wanted the carpet to turn the entire ensemble into a uniformly
designed whole. Its pattern therefore corresponded to Huszár's design.*

Piet Zwart

Colour draft for the sitting room carpet at the
Villa *De Arendshoeve*, Voorburg, 1921
*Kleurontwerp voor het tapijt in de zitkamer van
"De Arendshoeve" in Voorburg*
Gouache and collage on cardboard,
32.5 x 46 cm
Gemeentemuseum, The Hague

Huszár designed the colour scheme on the basis of Vincent van Gogh's famous *Bedroom in Arles* of 1889, which he redrew as the interplay of various bright and lively colours and elementary, usually rectangular shapes. He decomposed the original planes into asymmetrically arranged rectangles of different sizes and then applied the same principle to the colour of the furniture. The niches of the irregular rooms also served the purpose of accommodating the correspondence between the function and form of the beds and the washbasins. The large window mediated between these two planes that lay opposite one another, while at the same time providing a separating light zone.

Huszár used the large colour planes to cover up the fragmentation of the room and to emphasize or de-emphasize the various objects. The furniture was given dark colours, so that its shapes, which also consisted mainly of large rectangles, complemented the system of interdependent surfaces. The chairs and bedside table were painted wine-red and the linear elements of the frames black. The blue upholstery of the chairs was integrated into the general scheme by means of black bands sewn onto them, whereas the bedside table with its asymmetrically-placed black and red planes echoed the mural decoration on a smaller

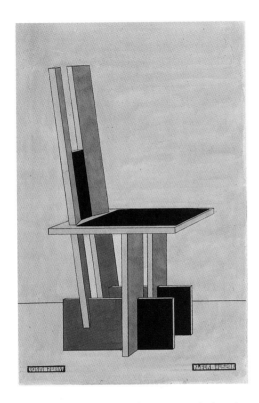

Piet Zwart (design) and Vilmos Huszár (colours)

Draft for a chair 1920
Ontwerptekening voor een stoel
Ink and watercolour, 51.3 x 34 cm
Gemeentemuseum, The Hague

Gerrit Rietveld

Red/Blue Chair, 1918–1923
Rood-blauwe leunstoel
Painted beechwood, 88 x 68 x 64 cm
Stedelijk Museum, Amsterdam

scale. Because of its vivid colours the room must have made a very cheerful impression, much more than that of an ordinary room. Huszár reinforced this aspect even further by arranging the colours so that they ran against each other. On the one side, for example, the walls above the beds were painted grey, with white planes fixed to them. The facing walls were the exact opposite: the remaining areas were painted white, with blue and yellow planes. The ceiling in the small side room was also painted blue, interrupted only by white bands. Unlike van Doesburg's early colour designs for rooms, this system did not keep very closely to the architectural conditions, but provided a conscious contrast by virtue of its large colour planes, which constituted a formative force of their own. This idea was to become extremely important to *De Stijl*.

Huszár was also involved in the design of other rooms at *De Arendshoeve*. The sitting room of 1921 (p. 118), for example, was quite typical. Apart from the conventional armchair, a number of items are particularly worth noting, i.e. several tables, upright chairs and the carpet.[124] The so-called smoking table and a side table were built according to a system of interlocking hollow cubes and interpenetrating planes. This was more than an application of the *De Stijl* principle of volumetric dissolution. It opened up possibilities for different functions: the partitions could be used as shelves. A carpet with irregularly distributed planes formed a basis which corresponded to the different sections on the walls. The composition was similar to that of a painting, so that it also provided a setting for the furniture, which necessarily appeared rather small by comparison, and rounded off the entire ensemble. The chair was a remarkable work of art. With its shape designed by Zwart and the colours by Huszár, it also followed the principle of interlocking planes and consisted of no more than eight wide and narrow boards of different sizes, forming the back, the supports, the seat and the legs. In this way the importance of stability was ideally combined with the simplicity of the material, so that its form displayed an amazing degree of clarity. The chair was also intended for mass production.[125]

Piet Zwart had learnt this method of furniture design from Klaarhamer, who had taught courses in Utrecht and developed his style from folk traditions. The first progressive forms of furniture also owe their existence to another artist who was subsequently extremely important for *De Stijl*. This was the cabinet maker and architect Gerrit Rietveld, another student of Klaarhamer's.[126] He had attended Klaarhamer's evening classes from 1911 to 1915 and also made furniture for him. Around the year 1917 he was commissioned to design furniture for *Verloop House*, built by Robert van 't Hoff, in Huis ter Heide, following drafts by Frank Lloyd Wright.[127] Although Rietveld only ever encountered Theo van Doesburg and *De Stijl* in 1919, when he responded to a critique of his furniture, it is likely that van der Leck was at least vaguely familiar with this new type of design, because he had also had contacts with Klaarhamer. This probably explains why his furniture reflected *De Stijl* ideas as early as 1918.

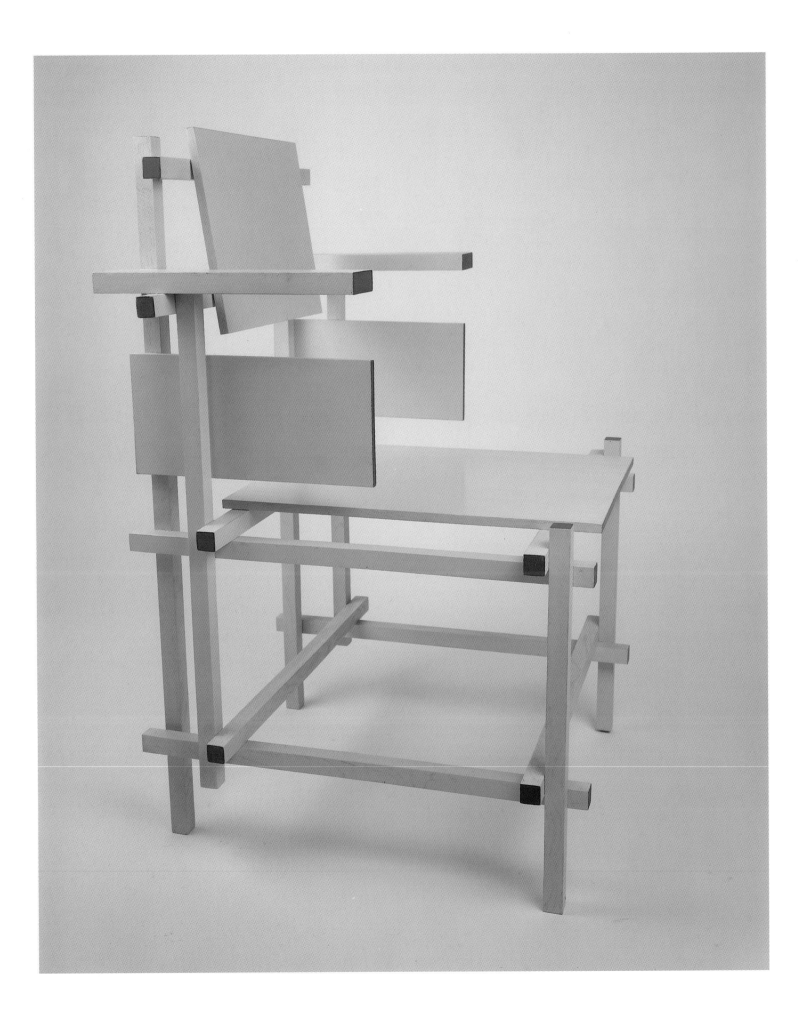

p. 122:
Gerrit Rietveld

High Chair, 1919
Oak, painted white and blue, 60 x 60 x 93 cm
Friedman Gallery, New York

p. 123:
Gerrit Rietveld

Children's Chair, 1920
Beechwood, leather seat and back,
45 x 40 x 90 cm
Friedman Gallery, New York

Gerrit Rietveld and his staff outside his workshop
in Adriaan van Ostadelaan in Utrecht,
photographed in 1918
*Rietveld is sitting in the prototype of what was
later called the Red/Blue Chair.*

Gerrit Rietveld

Prototype of the so-called
Red/Blue Chair, 1918
Beechwood, 87 x 60 x 60 cm
Friedman Gallery, New York

His famous *Red/Blue Chair* (p. 121) had already been designed in 1918, though it was not until 1923 that it was given its final form and the characteristic colours from which it derived its name.[128]

The first versions still had side panels under the arm rests, and this was the form in which it appeared in *De Stijl* at first.[129] Rietveld continually improved the chair in the years that followed this first version, either by changing the material or the dimensions. Added to this, the *Rietveld Chair* or *Red/Blue Chair* never existed as an object, but only as a concept. The ones that were actually made at Rietveld's workshop and are known to us today all differ from one another with regard to materials and/or dimensions. Today's reproductions are arbitrary versions which nevertheless somehow correspond to the original simply because Rietveld never defined a normative standard. It is therefore mere speculation and indeed erroneous to assume that the chair was based on a dimensional grid and a modular system (similar to the grid pattern of the *De Stijl* artists). It always had been – and continued to be for the Rietveld workshop – a mere product of their craftsmanship!

In its most widespread version the chair was 34 inches (88 cm) high. It consisted of 13 pieces of squared timber, two arm rests, a seat and a back, all of them bought by Rietveld machine-cut and in ordinary, standard dimensions. His idea of a design was that it should be both rational and inexpensive, a principle which he also followed in his design for the *Rietveld Schröder House*. Construction and design – i.e. engineering and aesthetics – are equated with a minimum of visible creative effort, so we are given an impression of simplicity even though the system behind it is highly complex. The various parts are connected in such a way that the overall construction appears self-contained.

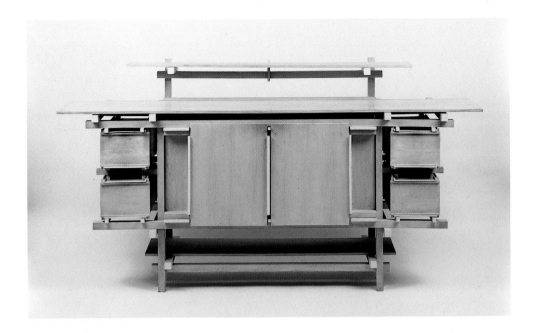

Gerrit Rietveld

Sideboard, 1919
Beechwood, painted with white aniline,
195 x 104 x 45 cm
Stedelijk Museum, Amsterdam

Gerrit Rietveld

Berlin Chair, 1923
Berlijnse stoel
Beechwood, painted black, medium grey, light
grey and white, 74 x 58 x 106 cm
Friedman Gallery, New York

Gerrit Rietveld

Side Table, 1923
Divantafeltje
Beechwood, painted red, blue, yellow, black and
white, 50 x 50 x 59.5 cm
Reproduction by Cassina di Meda

However, to ensure that no clearly delineated space is created, the elements are locked into each other without flush joints. Each part protrudes beyond the particular configuration to which it belongs.

The complexity of the construction is matched by its engineering principles: instead of fitting the wooden elements into one another, Rietveld fixed them alongside and on top of each other, fastening them with dowels in pre-drilled holes. The only places where Rietveld used screws were the seat and the back, i.e. surfaces that were subject to strain. This system, which seems to contradict our expectations of the structural distribution of load and support, was not entirely Rietveld's invention, but the logical further development from older engineering principles. Rietveld merely applied them to his dialectical concept of form.

Later, when colour was added, Rietveld used the characteristic *De Stijl* tones. However, these colours were not used in a purely decorative way, but in agreement with the principles of construction. All the parts of the squared timber frame are black and their squared-off surfaces yellow. The seat, on the other hand, was painted a heavy, solid blue, while the back, which was intended to support a load, was given an aggressive red.

With this dialectical construction Rietveld applied the basic principle of *De Stijl* art – the harmonization of opposites in the transcendence of space – and created a perfect structure that is more than a piece of furniture. Like *De Stijl* architecture, whenever it is consistent, it is above all a sculptural object. Unlike any other item, this chair unites elements of both formal and functional *De Stijl* ideals. It is both a work of art and an object for daily use, thus demonstrating the utopian vision of a different, yet ideal way of modelling the environment. It was the concrete rendering of a utopian idea, which explains why van Doesburg was so enthusiastic about it, hailing it as an excellent example of *De Stijl* art.[130]

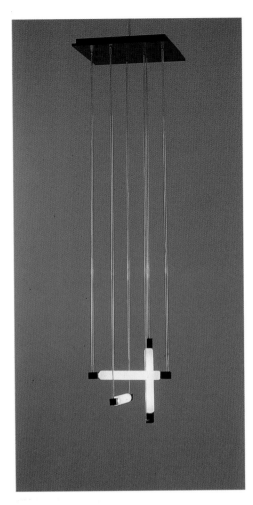

Gerrit Rietveld

Hanging Lamp, 1922
Incandescent bulbs and oak,
35 x 35 x 130 cm (variable height)
Modern reproduction by Cassina di Meda, man-
ufactured under licence by Tecta, Lauenförde

Rietveld subsequently continued to experiment with the dialectical principle of interlocking elements and designed a whole range of furniture items along these lines. His *Sideboard* was designed in 1919.[131] Although its construction resembled that of a conventional sideboard, its frame was made from vertical and horizontal squared timber, just like Rietveld's armchair of 1918/23. The timber was then combined with sections that seemed like two-dimensional planes. Like the *Red/Blue Chair*, this sideboard combines closed and open forms, as well as compact forms and those that extend into space.

Rietveld, who was totally undogmatic about shape, continually subjected his basic idea to further developments. In 1923/24, for example, he also designed chairs with rounded instead of squared timber, though he used dowels on them in the same way. The result was that the form of these chairs appeared to dissolve even further: the armchairs look as if the bars of wood are going to roll apart as soon as they are touched![132] A further radical development occurred – also in 1923 – when Rietveld began to construct completely asymmetrical furniture, largely by using flat wooden boards.

The prototype of this stage in the development was Rietveld's *Berlin Chair*, designed specially as a model for an exhibition in Berlin.[133] It is characterized by planar shapes that are consistently played off against linear ones, while at the same time changing functions. Compared with the armchair of 1918/23 this chair was rather more simplified: only eight elements were used altogether. There are two mirror-image versions, one facing left and the other right. Unlike Rietveld's early furniture, which was based on the principle of symmetrical construction, this chair has no axial harmony whatever. Whereas the struts that were cut from bars appeared either as lines or, when viewed from the side, as narrow planes, the boards are two-dimensional, but seem like linear elements when viewed from the side. Like a *De Stijl* painting, the chair gives the impression of a highly sensitive and delicately balanced structure, uniting numerous opposing forces.

The climax of this limitation to asymmetrical forms is the side table of the same year (1923).[134] Here only five elements are combined to form a piece of furniture, which is constructed entirely asymmetrically and, going against the stricter *De Stijl* norms, also has some rounded planes. While the *Berlin Chair* (p. 127) contains bright colours set in a colourless frame, with grey played off against black, the side table has a variety of colourful frames that have white surfaces set against black ones. The red base plate and the yellow edge at the top introduce a brightly colourful emphasis, counteracting all spatial/tectonic relationships.

Even nowadays this furniture seems like a radical and consistent artistic innovation, with a suggestive force that is unique, direct and persuasive, though – for the same reason – also extremely esoteric and hardly usable in daily life. Yet that was exactly its purpose. It was created not only as a result of a continuous dialogue with the ideals and manifestoes of *De Stijl*, but it also played an important part in the collaboration of *De Stijl* artists and interior designers.

Gerrit Rietveld

Interior and colour design for Dr. A. M. Hartog's
surgery, Maarssen, 1922
*Ruimte- en kleurcompositie voor de spreek-
kamer van Dr. A. M. Hartog*
Vintage photograph

Following the principles of his *Red/Blue Chair*, Rietveld also made
furniture for a room in Bart de Ligt's house in Katwijk aan Zee.[135] Van
Doesburg gave this irregularly shaped room a colour scheme with
large planes so that its three-dimensional character was neutralized for
the viewer.

In 1922 Rietveld designed the furniture and also the colour scheme
for the surgery of a general practitioner in Maarssen, Dr. Hartog. The
doctor's chair was a variation of the *High Chair* (p. 122), which was
already being used at Bart de Ligt's house, with a dark frame and white
squared-off edges, as well as a white seat and back. The colours of
another model of the same chair were the exact opposite. The room also
contained a box-like desk, a filing cabinet constructed in the same
manner as the lathwork chairs, a bed (not designed by Rietveld), an

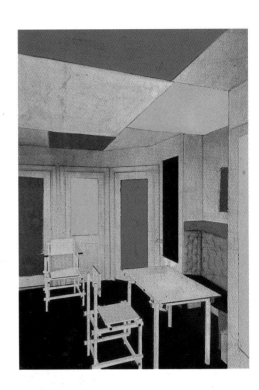

Theo van Doesburg

Colour design for a room in Bart de Ligt's house, Katwijk aan Zee, 1919-1924
Kleurontwerp voor een kamer in het huis van Bart de Ligt
Ink, gouache and collage, 27 x 21 cm
Rijksdienst Beeldende Kunst, The Hague

This is the corrected version of a colour scheme for a room, designed by van Doesburg in 1919. For publication in a magazine called L'architecture Vivante in autumn 1925, the artist changed the original composition from secondary colours to pure primary colours to give the false impression of a consistent De Stijl design. Among Gerrit Rietveld's furniture we can make out his so-called High Chair in the background (p. 122).

instrument case and two *Red/Blue Chairs*. The size of the room was 16 x 19 feet (5 x 6 metres), with white walls that had several grey and black planes. On the wall, beside the doctor's desk, Rietveld placed a large red sphere. Together with the design of the ceiling, this huge round mark helped to dissolve the given spatial limitations. The light was a remarkable construction: it consisted of two vertical and two horizontal incandescent bulbs with the power supply in separate, transparent little glass tubes. This caused quite a stir and is still being reproduced today.[136]

In 1921 Huszár and Wils designed a new studio for Henri Berssenbrugge, a photographer in The Hague.[137] Berssenbrugge, a member of the *Kunstkring* (Artists' Circle) in The Hague and a sponsor of the avantgarde, commissioned Wils to build him a long, rectangular room with a high ceiling behind his old reception hall. Huszár took care of the colour scheme. The ground was painted in two shades of grey and covered with black, blue and strawberry-red rugs. In conjunction with yellow-ochre stripes, these colour planes recurred on the walls, primed black and white, in large planes and set against one another. In this way correspondences were created that altered the spatial effect of the architectural conditions. This impression was further enhanced by Rietveld's furniture, consisting entirely of rectangular constructions with linear, cubic and planar effects. According to then contemporary press reports, the room was felt to be colourful, but not excessively so, and it was seen as extremely spacious and open.

Together with Piet Zwart, Wils also worked on the building and interior design of Gaillard and Jorissen's dancing school in The Hague. As the architect was able to design a completely new building and Zwart could decide on the interior, they were in fact working under ideal conditions. And yet the colour scheme, which may well have been enforced by the clients, was used in a far more constructional sense, i.e. in line with functional and architectural conditions rather than transcending them aesthetically.[138]

This confrontation between radical concepts of form and clients that were more interested in practicality and usefulness was a typical feature of *De Stijl* design as understood at the time. As a result, the ideas of *De Stijl* for industry were never fulfilled. Their drafts and works either remained confined to a small, exclusive group of clients or eventually merged with the International Style.

Ideas that were far ahead of the times, such as the concept behind the *Red/Blue Chair*, continue to be exclusive today, while others have undergone an indirect revival in the wake of totally new developments. This is what happened, for example, to a radio case (p. 133), designed by Rietveld together with Truus Schröder-Schräder in 1925.[139] The components which formed part of a then contemporary radio were built into a completely transparent rectangular glass construction that could be opened in different ways and moved around freely on three wheels. Avant-garde aesthetics consistently extended the contrast between the transparent glass and the self-exposing machinery of the radio – a method of design that went far beyond the times. While repairing the

Jan Wils (architecture) and Vilmos Huszár (colour design)

Berssenbrugge Photographic Studio, The Hague, 1921
Vintage photograph

radio, however, the electrician made a mistake and the whole fragile box fell to pieces. And so it never actually served its purpose and was never rebuilt either. Nowadays there are thousands of devices which are, in principle, very similar!

The same thing happened to Vilmos Huszár's design. In 1924 he succeeded in constructing a hanging lamp (p. 132), about 20 inches (50 cm) long, using sheets of glass which were at parallels and perpendicular. As a product design it far surpassed Rietveld's famous hanging lamp at Dr. Hartog's surgery. It was a perfect application of *De Stijl*'s current architectural ideas. Combining frosted glass and sheets of etched glass with each other, it achieved a new synthesis between the contrasts of transparence versus thickness and fragility versus function. However, it was never produced in series.[140] In subsequent years Huszár worked as a designer in a number of areas, designing, for example, furniture for Metz & Co.[141]

Vilmos Huszár

Hanging lamp, c. 1924
Vintage photograph

132

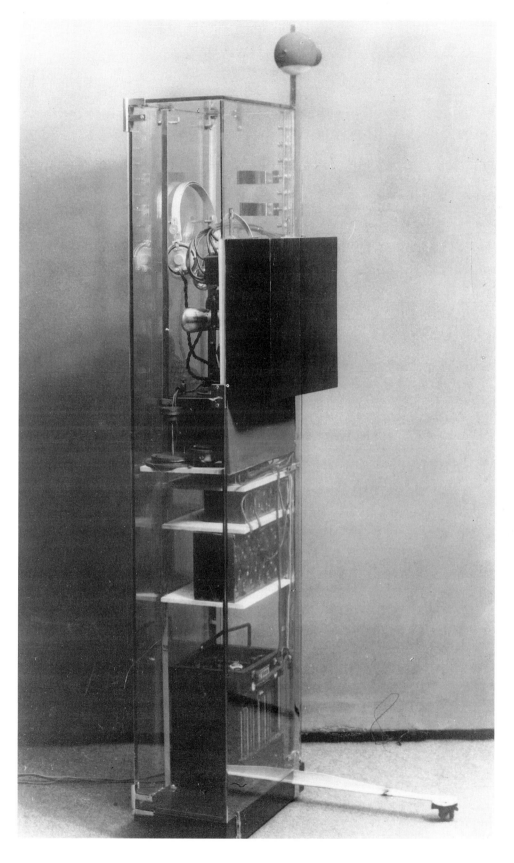

Gerrit Rietveld and Truus Schröder-Schräder

Glass case for a radio
Vintage photograph, 1925

133

Gerrit Rietveld demonstrating the model of a house designed by him
Photograph from the 1950s

And so *De Stijl* art was reflected in a variety of different spheres as a more or less radical design for everyday life, though nevertheless consistent with its own aesthetic principles. On the whole, this procedure eventually led to a general harmonization of the way in which shapes were formed.

The most distinct implementation of *De Stijl* principles can be seen in the *Rietveld Schröder House* in Utrecht, which was both planned and built in 1924.[142] Circumstances made it possible to realize the ideas of *De Stijl* architecture and design in a way that was truly unique. The client, Truus Schröder-Schräder, was an interior designer herself and took an active part in the planning. (In fact, she even joined *De Stijl*).[143] After her husband's death she no longer wanted to live in a big (and expensive) villa, but in a more functional house, together with her three children. The house is on Prins Hendriklaan at the end of a totally conventional row of terraced houses on what used to be the outskirts of Utrecht.

Technically, the building is far less revolutionary than its vocabulary of form might suggest.[144] Going against the *De Stijl* ideals, it was not built in reinforced concrete, but entirely of traditional materials. In fact, the architect used brick for the house itself and wood for the ceilings and the roof. Only the base of some of the balconies was made of exposed concrete. However, the walls were then plastered so that their real structure was consciously disguised. This underlined the impression of a continuous surface, and we are involuntarily reminded of concrete again. Rietveld accentuated the I-shaped iron profile mounts of the projecting supports for balconies and walls, as well as crossbeams and projections of the roof, as single horizontal and vertical elements, so that the construction became an autonomous shape. If he had used ferroconcrete, this would have been unnecessary and indeed mere mannerism. The use of iron girders was a novelty for residential houses at the time. The desired form was far more important than all considerations of civil engineering.

Rietveld designed the house with a view to its inside functions and the arrangement of the furniture. Then he made a model, and only when he had produced a number of tentative sketches and checked the dimensions did he carry out the projections for the exact construction plans. The final shape was always developed from a form that was cubic and self-contained at the beginning. Numerous changes were made in the process, and the final touches were in fact only added during the building stage. Rietveld was always conscious of the revolutionary nature of his building, and when he submitted his plans for building permission to the local authorities, he therefore marked the top floor – the most radical part of the house – as an attic.

The *Rietveld Schröder House* is the most resolute application of *De Stijl*'s principles of form. This is because it was designed and then built as an assembly of elements. The structural framework is provided by large, flat portions that were later painted white. Any spaces that were left empty were later filled with brickwork, so that a relationship between the inside and the outside was established. The sections were then painted white, and in four shades of grey. Defining horizontal and vertical accents, this system of lines was supplemented by the iron girders of the supports, the crossbeams and the gutter. They were painted white, black, grey, red and yellow. During assembly, apertures were left into which windows, the banister, a skylight roof window and the ladder were fitted from outside. These elements were painted black (window frames, banister and ladder), grey (window frames), blue (bench) and white (roof window/skylight).

Planes and lines were painted and assembled in such a way that their colours and sizes continued to be contrastive even when they were adjacent. Apart from the entrance door, which is not at the front but at the side, all doors and windows open outwards to allow more space within the building. The northeast-facing corner window on the top floor can be opened so that the corner itself disappears.

Open on three sides, the exterior view of the building is dominated by a significant difference between large and small planes. As a result, portions that face each other appear to be running in opposite directions. The left-hand half of the street front, which consists of the door and the window, is only interrupted by the balcony platform with its linear appearance. This half has a large white wall panel next to it on the right. The street front is matched at the back by a low white wall and the right-hand half with a door and windows, though on the top floor it also extends to the left.

In this way complementary relationships are built up without any symmetrical correspondences between them. The two functional elements – the chimney and the skylight – are not visible from the street level, so that they do not have an adverse effect on the impression of neutralized rectangles and surfaces placed above one another.

This diversity of the exterior is matched by the interior structure of the house, with functional areas arranged sequentially on each floor. At the street front there is a long rectangular studio which stretches towards the back. On its right, but set at right angles and thus leading towards the side front, is the study. Situated next to it is the entrance, at the side front. It leads into a small hallway and then a kitchen, which is almost square, and a staircase. The kitchen is adjacent to a room with windows and a windowless utility room. All the rooms are different in size and arranged around a fireplace that has been shifted away from the middle axis. The sequence of rooms on the top floor is a variation of this arrangement. There is a girls' bedroom above the studio, a boy's bedroom above the study, a sitting room above the kitchen and mother's bedroom with an adjoining bathroom above the back room and the windowless utility room.

However, the dimensions of the rooms on the upper floor do not correspond to the ones on the ground floor. Indeed there is a certain temporariness about them, due to wall partitions on slide rails. These walls can be folded so as to create a continuous room. By folding only some of the walls it is possible to divide the rooms into an almost infinite number of constellations. This is matched by the construction of the

Gerrit Rietveld

Rietveld-Schröder House, 1924
View from the street and looking towards the
entrance at the side,
50, Prins Hendriklaan, Utrecht

The Rietveld-Schröder House is like an assemblage of different-sized vertical and horizontal surfaces, put together in different ways. Achieving that typical De Stijl harmony between opposites, the exterior of the building seems composed and decomposed all at once. Characteristically, there is neither a main view nor a less important view of the house; all three sides are equally important. Behind the windows facing the street (Prins Hendriklaan) is a studio on the ground floor and the bedroom of Truus Schröder-Schräder's daughters on the top floor. Both rooms have a wall partition adjacent to them, with a study next to it downstairs and the son's bedroom upstairs. The windows of these rooms face the side of the entrance. On the other side we can see the kitchen windows downstairs and the windows of the big sitting room upstairs. This is the garden side. Adjoining these rooms is a small room on the ground floor and Truus Schröder-Schräder's bedroom on the top floor. The various opposites of the exterior are matched by the different distribution of rooms on the two floors. It is relatively conventional on the ground floor, with five self-contained living and function rooms as well as a hallway, whereas the top floor has a flexible floor plan, so that nearly all wall partitions can be changed or indeed removed altogether.

Rietveld-Schröder House, Utrecht, 1924
Ground floor

*Two views of the kitchen. The window facing the
entrance side has a special section for delivery-
men and, in front of it, three so-called Zig-Zag
Chairs from 1934, grouped around a table. The
work surface and the sink unit are on the left.
Below the window are the heating pipes that
were common in industry at the time. At the back
of the kitchen, under the glass sideboard, is a so-
called Military Chair from 1923, with a door
leading to the garden on the left. To the left of the
dumbwaiter is the door to the servant's room.*

Rietveld-Schröder House, Utrecht, 1924
Ground floor

A view of the study from the window on the entrance side. Behind the desk is Rietveld's chair of 1925 and in the left-hand corner, hardly noticeable, a washbasin. It is a characteristic feature of the Rietveld-Schröder House that every room has a washbasin.

Rietveld-Schröder House: flexible room arrangement on the top floor (see also pp. 88, 142 and 143).

The big sitting room has an upholstered sofa alongside the glass panel of the staircase, as well as a stove which was added later. Opposite the sofa we can see the speaking tube for communicating between the sitting room and the kitchen (p. 88), and in the background a view of the children's bedrooms. In the part of the sitting room that faces the garden are some foldable desks on the right, where the children used to do their homework, and between them the dining table. These different photographs illustrate the

principle of variable room distribution. Running along slide rails and consisting of several upright rectangular boards, the wall partitions can be folded to create a bigger room. However, it is also possible to put up all or some of them so that the children's bedrooms are then separated from the dining/sitting room.

Rietveld-Schröder House: view of the big dining/sitting room facing the garden, top floor.

The photograph on the left was taken in 1981, showing the interior during the last years of Truus Schröder-Schräder's life. In the background, on the left, next to the dining table, we can see Rietveld's so-called Steltman Chair of 1963.

One of our views (top right) shows a wall partition that is closed between the children's bedrooms but open towards the staircase. Mother's bedroom is also partitioned off in this way. Looking past the girls' beds, placed at right angles to each other, are the banister and a ladder mounted onto it which leads to the trap door in the skylight (access to the roof). We can also see the cupboard and the window in Truus Schröder-Schräder's bedroom. The other view (top left) shows the length of her son's bedroom on the side of the entrance as well as the balcony. Here the wall partition leading to the sitting/dining room is closed so that part of it can be moved like a door.

The entire room also contains several items of furniture designed by Rietveld, including the Little Divan Table, designed in 1923, the Red/Blue Chair of 1918-1923 and, together with the Military Chair, also the Ironing Chair of 1928, made from bent steel pipes and a curved wooden board.

This vintage photograph shows the interior of a home designed by Gerrit Rietveld and Truus Schröder-Schräder together. It belonged to the paediatrician Dr. Harrestein, whose wife An was Truus Schröder-Schräder's sister. Weteringschans, Amsterdam

hinge-framed beds and tables which can also be folded, put up or fastened to the walls. The colour design of the floors and the spaces between them is in black, white, grey and red. The blue walls accentuate the flexible structure of the entire arrangement. The building was originally heated by a series of pipes running through the house, the kind that were also common in industrial buildings.

What makes the *Rietveld Schröder House* such an interesting piece of contemporary architecture is not only its unusual exterior, but also the fact that it was the first building with flexible floor plans. These had been postulated by Theo van Doesburg and Cornelis van Eesteren in their architectural programme (cf. Chapter 6), where they also designed some examples of it.

As a unified concept which included both architectural and interior design, the *Rietveld Schröder House* was virtually unparalleled in the history of modern architecture. Radical avant-garde principles were combined with a coherent ensemble that was both practical and economical. Having developed his three-dimensinal design principle in his *Red/Blue Chair* (p. 121) of 1918 and then further in his *Berlin Chair* (p. 127) of 1923, Rietveld subsequently translated his ideas into architecture. Never again were *De Stijl* ideals applied so radically to actual buildings.

After Truus Schröder-Schräder's death in 1985, the building was renovated. It is now in the hands of a foundation and open to the public as a museum, owned by the Centraal Museum in Utrecht.

In the following years Rietveld was able to apply his principles to a number of projects. Together with Truus Schröder-Schräder he designed the interior of a flat in Weteringschans, Amsterdam, in 1926.[145] He turned a long, narrow room into an interior that could be used for cooking, leisure, meals and work. Only the bedroom was separated from this integrated area. Rietveld used the same furniture he had designed before; only a glass showcase was new.

In 1927, in Wassenaar, he built a house that was unfortunately destroyed soon afterwards. Although it was modelled on the *Rietveld Schröder House*, its dissolution of form was noticeably less obtrusive.[146] Of the projects of that time, a garage with a chauffeur's flat in Utrecht is particularly worth noting, a building that can still be viewed in its original state today (p. 146). What is surprising about this house is the use of prefabricated elements, a method that was far ahead of the time. The house is based on a construction of double steel girders and one-by-three metre cement slabs with perforated sheet-metal panels. At the same time, the entire cubic construction was dissolved into planar and linear elements, without reducing the constructional firmness and clarity of proportions.[147]

In 1930/31, while *De Stijl* still existed, Rietveld worked together with Truus Schröder-Schräder on a block of terraced houses on Erasmuslaan in Utrecht (p. 147), opposite the *Rietveld Schröder House*.[148] It followed a one-metre modular system and was given the flexible ground plan arrangement which had become so typical of Rietveld's style. The vertical structure of the three-storey block is crossed by the horizontal elements of the line of windows, as well as the long balcony and the wall section between the ground floor and the first floor.

However, these impressive implementations and further developments of *De Stijl* ideas must not obscure our view to the fact that they were never more than isolated occurrences at the time. *De Stijl* was by no means generally accepted in the Netherlands; nor did it have any leading position. This can be gathered from the considerable compromises which *De Stijl* artists had to make in order to carry out their ideas. The general public had great difficulties coming to terms with it, because most contemporaries felt that *De Stijl*'s vocabulary of form was excessively rational, cool and rigid.

Gerrit Rietveld

Lommer House, Wassenaar, 1927

Gerrit Rietveld

Garage with chauffeur's flat,
Utrecht, 1927

Dutch Expressionism, in particular, was far more popular at the time. The architects and designers of the so-called *Amsterdam School* — Michel de Klerk, Pieter Kramer, Mathieu Lauweriks and others — were given far more opportunity to put their ideas into practice, sometimes even in extremely large-scale projects. This was partly due to the support given to this movement by the authorities who commissioned such projects. Whereas *De Stijl* wanted to express utopian ideas in concrete terms and had an intellectual approach to their work, members of the *Amsterdam School* trusted in their intuition and tried to cater for the human need for warmth and comfort, especially in interior design.

This group found its mouthpiece in a magazine called *Wendingen* (i.e. 'changes'), and their vocabulary of form, which dated back to Art Nouveau, soon began to gain ground.[149] In the decade from 1920 to 1930 modern Dutch design was dominated by expressive buildings with traditional and, as it were, natural Dutch brickwork as well as decorative (nowadays often stuffy-looking) furniture and interior. As a result,

Gerrit Rietveld

Terraced houses on Erasmuslaan,
Utrecht, 1930

society had certain expectations which, to some extent, also affected projects of the *De Stijl* artists – for example, at Spangen.

Whenever revolutionary and aesthetically daring solutions to the problems of everyday design were given a chance, it was an exception. Piet Zwart succeeded in doing so in 1921 with an exhibition stand for a celluloid manufacturer (p. 148). After several, comparatively conventional attempts, he designed a series of shelves supported by a frame that consisted of vertical, horizontal and oblique wooden bars protruding into the surrounding space.

The principles of form, developed by Rietveld with his armchair of 1918, were obviously influential. In turn, however, Rietveld's furniture was also influenced by the colour scheme of an exhibition stand, designed by Zwart in 1923: he used black for the supporting elements, yellow for the ends of the bars, which were marked like squared-off surfaces, and blue, red and yellow for the diagonal and vertical supports. The arrangement was put up in such a way that the black, white

147

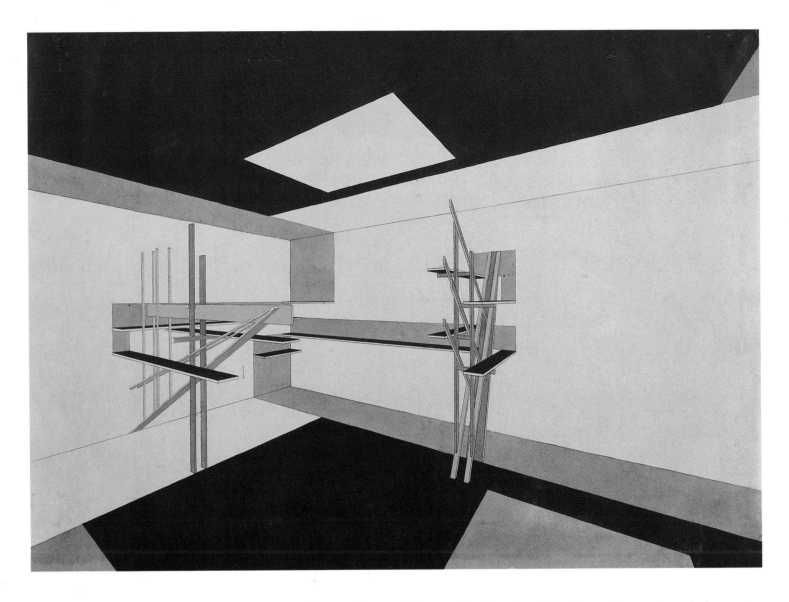

Piet Zwart

Design of an exhibition stand for a celluloid
manufacturer, 1921
*Ontwerp voor de beursstand van de celluloid-
fabriek*
Ink and gouache, 45.7 x 64.7 cm
Gemeentemuseum, The Hague

and grey planes of the walls disguised the three-dimensional character
of the display. The visitor was meant to become part of the structure of
the stand, so that he was directly confronted with the exhibits.[150]

Between 1920 and 1922 Rietveld himself established a dialectical
relationship between radical form and practical function in his design
of a jeweller's shop on Kalverstraat in Amsterdam (p. 150).[151] The relationship consisted entirely of an accumulation of parallel, flat bodies
and colourful rectangular surfaces that were at different angles, though
they added up to a coherent picture.

He placed large glass showcases at the front, running in opposite
directions. These were matched by a long and narrow rectangular box
on the left, at the back, reversing the relationships of the first level. The
spatial change was further accentuated by the colour of the showcases:
the front cases were painted red, the ones behind them, on the left and
right, were blue and the ones at the back yellow. Their bright colours
neutralized the colourless bars which were painted black, grey and
white. The same principle was repeated for the showcases, cupboards
and carpets inside the shop, so that a unified structure was achieved.

Cornelis van Eesteren

Perspective draft for a shopping arcade with a
café-restaurant, The Hague, 1924
*Perspektiefontwerp voor een winkelgalerij met
café-restaurant*
Pencil, ink, tempera and collage on cardboard,
52.7 x 51.3 cm
Nederlands Documentatiecentrum voor de
Bouwkunst, Amsterdam
Stichting van Eesteren-Fluck-Van Lohuizen

Vilmos Huszár

Poster for the exhibition *Industrial Design*, 1929
*Affiche voor de tentoonstelling van "Heden-
dagsche Kunstnyverheid"*
Lithograph, 69.9 x 59.7 cm
Stedelijk Museum, Amsterdam

Vilmos Huszár's oeuvre shows, par excellence, how practicalities can lead to artistic imbalance. Although he was often able to use progressive typography and composition in individual posters – such as his poster for an industrial design exhibition at the Stedelijk Museum in Amsterdam in 1929 [152] – other works were subject to his client's requirements so that their general effect was less consistent. This can be seen in the advertising campaign for *Miss Blanche* cigarettes.[153]

Huszár was responsible for the entire product design during the 1926/27 advertising campaign, from the company's stationery to the outdoor publicity posters. Both the typographical devices and the typical feature of a stylized smoking woman largely followed current conventions. Any visual ideas that approached *De Stijl* ambitions were confined to the Egyptian cigarettes of this brand, apparently because the advertisers could exploit a certain similarity between people's expectations towards Egyptian art and *De Stijl* abstraction.

It was not until the victory of International Style that *De Stijl* forms actually gained wider acceptance. This development was helped by Theo van Doesburg's single-minded endeavours to promote the international prestige of *De Stijl*.

Gerrit Rietveld

Shop of the Gold and Silversmith Company on Kalverstraat, Amsterdam, 1921
Winkel van de Goud- en Zilversmidcompagnie
Vintage photograph

ET AAA
B·N·A
K·V·B·
V·N·K
25
JAAR

1999

TENTOONSTELLING

van HEDENDAAGSCHE
KUNSTNYVERHEID
KLEINPLASTIEK
ARCHITECTUUR

STEDELYK MUSEUM
AMSTERDAM
29·JUNI — 28·JULI
GEOPEND van 10-5
INGERICHT door den TENTOONSTELLINGS
RAAD voor BOUWKUNST en VERWANTE KUNSTEN

V. HUSZAR

Group photograph of the delegates at the International Constructivists' Conference in Weimar in 1922. Theo van Doesburg: wearing a bowler hat, black shirt and light tie; El Lissitzky: in the same row, wearing a peaked cap.

6: " ... Creative Inter-nationalism ..." [154]

De Stijl cover from the first issue of the first year, January 1921, until the commemorative issue for Theo van Doesburg in January 1932

In the same way that *De Stijl* was not restricted to any particular artistic genre, it was not narrowly confined to its national borders, either. The magazine itself, of course, was started in the Netherlands, where it was published and supported by a group of mainly Dutch artists.

But this was really only true of the first years. The situation changed completely when most members of the first hour had turned away from *De Stijl* and Theo van Doesburg. Van Doesburg's endeavours were increasingly directed at the international scene, and artists from different European countries began to find a mouthpiece in *De Stijl*. Wherever new forms of art reached the public, *De Stijl* was there, too – or was at least trying to put in an appearance. Thus the magazine became a platform for discussions of rationalist, abstract art that went beyond national borders and transcended different artistic styles.

De Stijl changed its face, though without betraying the ideals of its first years. The most important theoretical contribution, apart from Mondrian's essay *Neo-Plasticism in Painting*, was the article on Italian Futurism by Gino Severini, *Painting of the Avant-garde*, which was published in French.[155] His convictions can be summarized in his motto: "Constructing a machine is like constructing a work of art."[156] Van Doesburg responded by publishing Oud's essay "Art and Machine" in the next issue. From the very beginning *De Stijl* had published the works of other modern art movements, with a view to discussing and analyzing them and regarding them either as worth following or rejecting them as misguided. The works of *De Stijl* artists were placed alongside Picasso's Cubist paintings, Archipenko's sculptures, Frank Lloyd Wright's buildings and many others. Although *De Stijl* seemed to have some rather dogmatic manifestoes, the artists and propagandists of the movement were always open to new ideas.

From 1921 onwards Theo van Doesburg propagated *De Stijl* nearly everywhere in Europe, and the magazine continually changed its format, cover and layout, proudly showing "Leiden – Antwerp – Paris – Rome" as its places of publication (in complete contradiction to its relatively low circulation).[157] However, this was by no means a break with its own past or ideals, but – initially – a desperate reaction to a deep-rooted crisis.

Van Doesburg was virtually on his own. Only Mondrian still maintained contact, and Rietveld, who had only recently joined, did not make any theoretical contributions at all. If, in 1921, I.K. Bonset, Aldo Camini and Theo van Doesburg published articles on modern poetry, abstract film, a new philosophy of life and aphoristic statements (for example on suicide and kleptomania),[158] then this was in fact a mere soliloquy. Behind all these names was one and the same person: Christian Emil Marie Küpper alias Theo van Doesburg. It was his way of trying to maintain the image of the movement. If, until then, the magazine *De Stijl* had been published regularly, it only appeared sporadically from now on. Van Doesburg, however, began to appear himself.

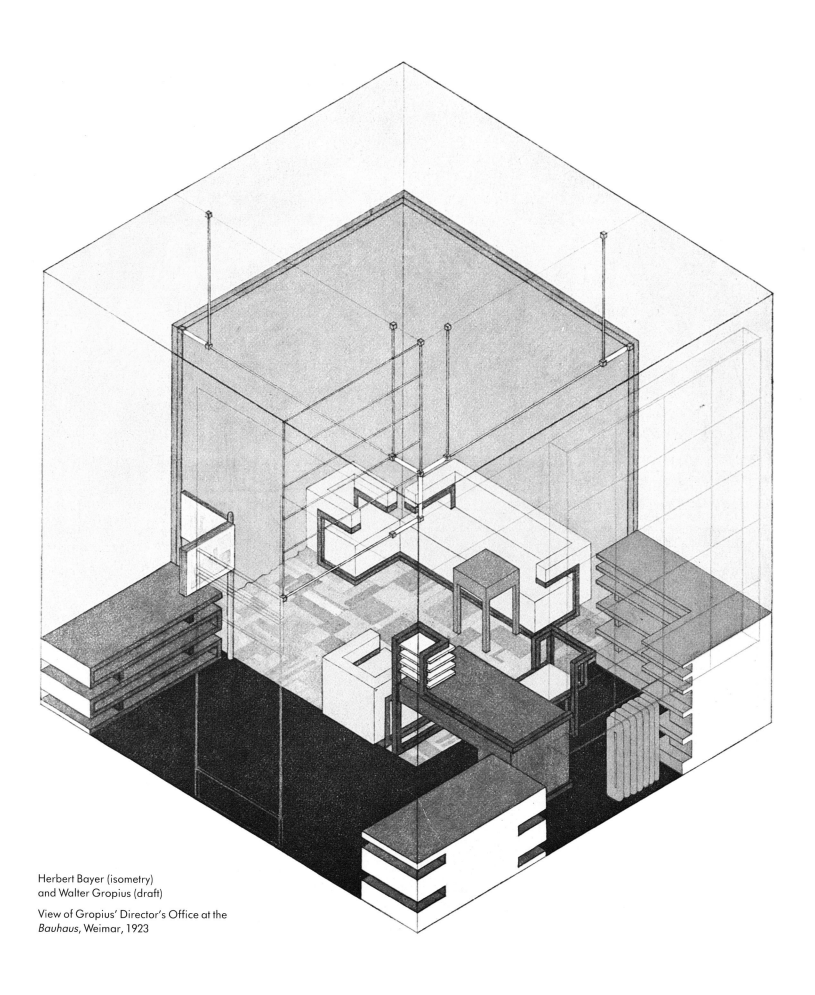

Herbert Bayer (isometry)
and Walter Gropius (draft)

View of Gropius' Director's Office at the
Bauhaus, Weimar, 1923

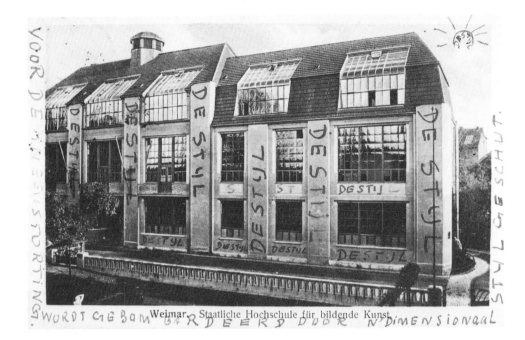

Theo van Doesburg

Bauhaus, conquered by *De Stijl*
On 12 September 1921 van Doesburg sent a postcard of the *Bauhaus* building in Weimar to Anthony de Kok, with *De Stijl* written over it.

In this way he did indeed manage to turn *De Stijl* into a major force in the development of classical modernism. The first significant step in his new undertaking was the German *Bauhaus* in Weimar. Following an invitation by Viking Eggeling and Hans Richter, two artists who had developed abstract motion pictures, van Doesburg visited Berlin in December 1920, where he met several important figures in German Modernism: the Bauhaus director Walter Gropius, his colleagues and assistants Adolf Meyer and Fred Forbat, and the architect Bruno Taut. At Taut's house van Doesburg gave a slide show on *De Stijl* art.

Having obtained a flat through Adolf Meyer, beneath Paul Klee's, van Doesburg paid a number of visits to Weimar in 1921 and 1922, during which time he tried to exert his influence on daily life and art at the *Bauhaus*.[159] He felt that its orientation was far too irrational for Modernism.[160] In fact, van Doesburg caused upheaval and unrest at the *Bauhaus*. He himself described this time as a period of reorientation of their training programme – a claim he documented visibly in the form of a postcard to Anthony Kok, on which he wrote *De Stijl* on all the walls of the *Bauhaus*.[161]

This claim, however, was contradicted by van Doesburg's low official standing at the *Bauhaus*. In particular, he failed to attain the status of a "Meister". Gropius prevented this from happening.[162] Nevertheless, van Doesburg's appearance did influence the students at the college. He offered a course outside regular teaching hours, directed above all against Johannes Ittens' introductory lectures, which he considered to be rather confused. The aim of this course was to teach the basics of architectonic design. The extent to which his classes were appreciated can be gathered from comments by other *Bauhaus* artists who would have loved van Doesburg as a colleague on the regular teaching staff.[163] Van Doesburg's rationalism was therefore an important element in the development of the *Bauhaus*, leading away from the almost romantic beginnings which had expressed themselves in their return to the structures of mediaeval stonemason's lodges. The elements of architecture as developed by van Doesburg, the reduction of the building space to simple cubic, planimetric and, as it were, sculptural forms in order to experiment with fundamental relationships between shapes – all this was quite similar to the methods which also characterized the teaching of the *Bauhaus* students.[164] Van Doesburg's undeniable success must therefore be seen not so much in the innovations he is supposed to have introduced, but in his greater rationality and, above all, external circumstances. The works of art and fundamental theories of *De Stijl* were already well-known and in use. In 1921 the *Bauhaus* only lacked one element that should in fact have been of central importance: it did not have any courses in architecture! Van Doesburg was therefore filling a gap.[165]

The extent to which *Bauhaus* "Meisters" assimilated and creatively modified *De Stijl* ideas can be seen in Gropius himself, whose director's office (p. 155) was furnished with items he himself designed.[166] The basic shape of the room was a square, and the isometric projection by Herbert Bayer, who was a lecturer at the Bauhaus in graphic design, shows that all the parts of the room were based on this pattern. Similar to *De Stijl*, the individual details were brought together by developing planar and spatial relationships from the lines, borders and planes that form part of a square. These were then enhanced plastically in the form of a cube.

Although there is no typical *De Stijl* colour scheme that would dissolve the dimensions of space within this ensemble, its influence is nevertheless noticeable in small details such as the lighting system, which is a variation of the Rietveld lamps in Dr. Hartog's surgery room in Maarssen (p. 129). Furthermore, essays by *De Stijl* artists Mondrian, van Doesburg and Oud were published in a series of *Bauhaus* books in 1925 and 1926.[167]

Developments in the art world were rather stormy during these years, and events succeeded one another very fast. Even during the *De Stijl* course in Weimar, van Doesburg took part in the International Congress of Progressive Artists, organized by El Lissitzky, from 29 to 31 May, 1922.[168] The meeting was attended by a large number of different artists' groups and movements, and there was a tendency towards forming two major camps, of which the one was more Constructivist in orientation and the other more Expressionist, or "impulsivist" as a report in *De Stijl* described it.[169]

The Dutch *De Stijl* movement thus came into contact with the German *G* group, the Italian Futurists, *L'Effort Moderne* from Paris, the *Sept Arts* circle from Brussels, Constructivist groups from Romania, Switzerland, Germany and Scandinavia, as well as Dadaists and independent artists. Together with others, El Lissitzy, Theo van Doesburg and the Constructivists formed a so-called International Constructivists' Faction. In autumn Van Doesburg then organized a Constructivists' Congress in Weimar.[170]

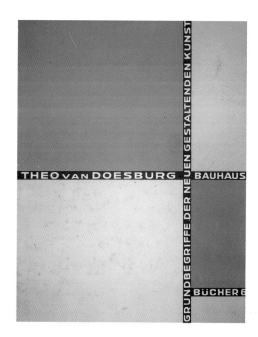

Front covers of the two *Bauhaus* books by Piet Mondrian and Theo van Doesburg

El Lissitzky

Proun BGA No. 4, 1923
Oil on canvas, 77 x 82 cm
Gemeentemuseum, The Hague

For the magazine *De Stijl*, which was still pretending to represent a lively Dutch movement, this period meant an intensive discussion of Soviet avant-garde art. El Lissitzky's *Proun* objects and rooms expressed similar artistic intentions for *De Stijl*.[171] In 1923 El Lissitzy designed a *Proun* room for the Greater Berlin Art Exhibition, which was reconstructed at the Van Abbe Museum in Eindhoven in 1965.[172] Like Huszár, Rietveld and van Doesburg, he took the dissolution of space with "lines, planes, sticks, cubes, spheres, black, white, grey and wood" – motifs in painting that had been developed in the *Proun* drawings and prints – and applied it to interior design.[173] In particular, El Lissitzky wanted to abolish the wall as a "resting place for... pictures" and enliven it. The fundamental similarities with *De Stijl* works were quite obvious, particularly with Piet Zwart's arrangement of the exhibition stand in 1921 (p. 148). Lissitzky, however, developed this system further, so that it was no longer tied to a function, but became a completely abstract arrangement.

El Lissitzky

Proun Room, designed for the Greater Berlin Art
Exhibition, 1923
Reconstruction, coloured wood,
300 x 300 x 260 cm
Stedelijk Van Abbe Museum, Eindhoven

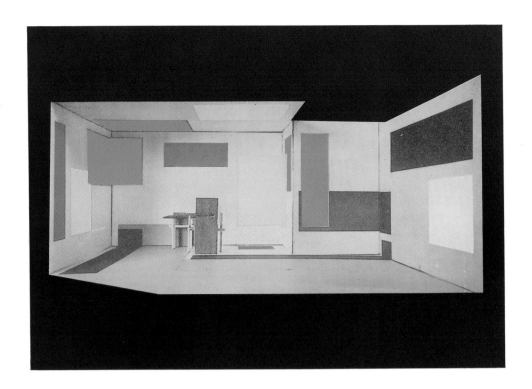

Vilmos Huszár (design)
and Gerrit Rietveld (execution)

Model of a room for the Greater Berlin Exhibition 1923, after the illustration in *L'architecture vivante*, 1924, plate 10.

Parallel with Lissitzky's projects, the *De Stijl* artists Rietveld and Huszár also achieved an abstract spatial concept that was to be realized and displayed at the Greater Berlin Art Exhibition in 1923.[174] Any designs that were not executed were shown in the form of models. Huszár contributed the colour scheme and Rietveld the construction. He also designed the *Berlin Chair* (p. 127) for this occasion. The exhibition room had six walls. An arrow showed the visitor which way he was meant to go. A small corridor with black, white and grey planes led to a larger room in which colour planes in all primary colours as well as black, white and grey overlapped one another and traversed the corners. Together with the furniture, this had the effect of neutralizing the walls, while changing and transcending the dimensions. In an interior of this kind Rietveld's chair became a sculpture, because its shape and colours corresponded exactly to the general design principle of the room.

Photograph of the exhibition *Les architects du groupe De Stijl* at the *L'Effort Moderne* Gallery in Paris, 1923.

In the foreground we can see the model of the Maison Rosenberg, *behind it on the right the model of the* Maison d'Artiste, *in the middle of the room on the left a model and axonometric projections of the* Maison particulière. *The designs are by Cornelis van Eesteren and Theo van Doesburg. On the wall: Oud's plans for the Purmerend factory (p. 115).*

The climax of all important tendencies in the development of *De Stijl* was an exhibition of architectural models and drafts in Paris towards the end of 1923. It was organized by Léonce Rosenberg, who had already published contributions in *De Stijl* in 1920/21. For a month, works by Theo van Doesburg, Cornelis van Eesteren, Jacobus Johannes Pieter Oud, Willem van Leusden, Vilmos Huszár, Gerrit Rietveld, Mies van der Rohe, Jan Wils and Piet Zwart were shown at his *L'Effort Moderne* gallery, from 15th October to 15th November. This made it partly a retrospective exhibition, presenting *De Stijl* as a homogeneous group and uniting artists who were not – or no longer – working together.[175] On the other hand, it also pointed towards the future. Mies van der Rohe was a German artist who belonged to the *G* group at the time, and who later became the director of the *Bauhaus* and achieved world fame as one of the pioneers of International Style. The exhibition included his plans for a skyscraper.

Vintage photograph of *Maison Rosenberg* model, designed by van Eesteren and van Doesburg. Entrance and garden sides.

Oud participated with seven exhibits, including a perspective draft for the Purmerend Factory (p. 115). Rietveld included a model of a showcase for the jeweller's shop on Kalverstraat in Amsterdam, and he had also built the model for one of van Doesburg and van Eesteren's architectural projects (*Maison Rosenberg*). Huszár and Zwart contributed, among other things, the design for a draft of a women's residence. An exhibition catalogue was published, showing 17 works and mentioning 52 exhibits (models, drafts, etc.).[176] The opening of the exhibition was attended by a large number of important artists, including Fernand Léger and Le Corbusier.

The exhibition had a good propaganda effect and succeeded in giving the Parisian public an understanding of Dutch *De Stijl* as something that was lively, creative and varied. But its importance in art history lay above all in the models and drafts designed by Theo van Doesburg and Cornelis van Eesteren together. Although the comments of contemporary French architects – especially Le Corbusier – sounded rather skeptical, the axonometric projections and architectural principles of these models nevertheless became influential.

Van Eesteren and van Doesburg were showing new designs for three projects: the house of the gallery owner Rosenberg, and two houses with no particular clients in mind – a model of a private house and one of a studio and residential house for an artist.[177] The most traditional of these projects was the one for Léonce Rosenberg.[178] It was a large, spacious complex. The house itself had three floors, with a conventional front and back, as well as bedrooms and living rooms separated on different levels.

Theo van Doesburg and Cornelis van Eesteren
working on a model for the *Maison particulière*

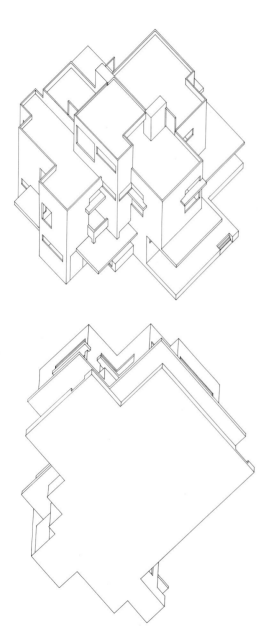

Theo van Doesburg and Cornelis van Eesteren

Axonometric projection of the
Maison particulière, 1923
Phototype, 57 x 57 cm
Axonometric projection (seen from below) of the
Maison particulière, 1923
Pencil and ink, 60.4 x 58.2 cm
Rijksdienst Beeldende Kunst, The Hague

The premises also included a gallery, a garage, a garden with sports facilities and a conservatory which linked the gallery and the house. The top floors of the house also provided space for a gymnastics and shower room and several terraces. Léonce Rosenberg had outlined his ideas of the distribution and functions of the various rooms in a number of sketches. Van Eesteren and van Doesburg then created an L-shaped complex consisting of several adjacent blocks with large gaps for the windows, protrusions and recesses. Although it was not as self-contained as Rosenberg had envisaged, it was nevertheless characterized by the principle of firm contours.

By contrast, when the artists were working on the *Maison particulière*, their most ambitious project, they defined a firm nucleus as a focal point.[179] The rooms were arranged freely around the stairway on a continuous level of 360-degrees. The volume of the building was not fixed in advance. Instead, the architects started with a rough idea of the overall space to which the volume was then adapted. Form and function were treated as inextricably linked, so that each room could be assigned a certain size and shape, depending on its purpose, without making these parameters dependent on the adjacent rooms. As a result, the house was not built from the outside to the inside, but the other way round, starting from inside and reaching outwards. Consequently the exterior was not dominated by any one particular view. It did not have the traditional four sides of a building, but the overall shape was determined by a variety of different perspectives. The nucleus, the terraces and the gymnastics room had three floors, like the *Maison Rosenberg*. Entrances, access to the garage, most hallways and the servants' quarters were situated in the northern parts of the building, and two floors in the southern half had sitting rooms, studies, bedrooms and terraces with interlocking sides. The entire arrangement can be regarded as cross-shaped, particularly in view of the tower-like stairwell, with a basic shape that was eroded and decomposed by the presence of interlocking volumes. This made the *Maison particulière* an innovation – unique and ahead of its time – based on the playful use of traditional shapes.

The drafts show that an extremely important element in this hitherto unexecuted project was to be the colour scheme. Using only primary colours, black and white, van Doesburg would have done more to the building than paint it. These colours would have penetrated it, because the colour planes would have been totally unrelated to the architectonic planes. Some colour planes would have covered the walls only in parts, while at the same time traversing into other rooms. It was the logical further development of van Doesburg's earlier ideas. He felt that architecture should develop from a building with a certain amount of space, detached from its surroundings, to a spatial arrangement of planes, grouped together in a flexible way.

Their third project, the *Maison d'Artiste*, was different again. It had four floors and, in addition to the usual rooms, included a large studio extending over two floors as well as a spacious sitting room.[180]

164

Theo van Doesburg and Cornelis van Eesteren

Axonometric projection of the
Maison particulière, 1923
Ink, gouache, collage, 57 x 57 cm
Rijksdienst Beeldende Kunst, The Hague

The three axonometric projections show the
Maison particulière *from a viewpoint diagonally
above and below. The colour study shows the
residential areas above the functional sections*
*(below), with the kitchen and bathroom/toilet on
the ground floor. Rising above the two-storeyed
sections with terraces is a third floor which has a
sports and gymnastics room, as well as a shower
room, in addition to the stairwell. The view from
below shows the opposite portion of the sections
which are at right angles. These include a big
lounge and a study on the ground floor as well as
bedrooms on the top floor. The third axonometric*
*projection gives a view of the corner that links
the two opposite sides, i.e. the functional and
residential sections. On the ground floor is a garage and a big cloakroom next to the entrance.
The office with the terrace, partly under a roof, is
on the right, and the terrace also extends around
the corner and along the lounge.*

Theo van Doesburg

Counter-construction of the *Maison particulière*,
1924
Contra-constructie
Pencil, ink, gouache and collage, 54.5 x 40.5 cm
Rijksdienst Beeldende Kunst, The Hague

*Based on the axonometric projections which van
Doesburg had designed together with Cornelis
van Eesteren, he then developed counter-constructions whose principle can be seen in these
two studies of the same corner of the building.
We are looking at the terrace side of the house
from above, i.e. the place where the two sections
join together. These sections have a study and a
big lounge on their ground floors, respectively.
Van Doesburg designed these partly roof-cov-
ered terraces in such a way that they were detached from their architectural context. He did
this by splitting up their forms or extending them
into the interior of the building. In the same way,
he also split up the other walls and created new
planar figures and cubes. When the artist added
colour, he went one step further, defining certain
sections with various primary and colourless
planes, which then penetrated the overall context
of the building while at the same time creating
space.*

The basic principle is the same as for the *Maison particulière*. Again, rooms were understood in terms of their shape and form and were then grouped around a stairwell that served as the nucleus. The individualization of rooms had gone even further here, but the colour scheme was closely related to the architectonic planes. The model was produced by a plumber who used welded lead frames. All planar surfaces therefore appear framed, thus giving special emphasis to their different colours.

It is obvious that the architect was inspired by Mondrian's pictorial compositions and their characteristic arrangement of colours and lines. The houses were to be built of reinforced concrete so that the free development of form would have been reflected in the civil engineering aspect as well. Yet they were not as radical as other contemporary designs, such as Mies van der Rohe's country houses, published in the magazine *G* in 1923.[181] It was based on an open ground plan, with walls dividing up the rooms and a far more consistent interdependence of the exterior and interior. Thus Frank Lloyd Wright's postulate was met in which he had demanded that the house should no longer be a mere box. It is worth noting van Doesburg's policy: although he was quite happy to include van der Rohe as a representative of a related German artists' group at the *De Stijl* exhibition, he did not allow him to show designs which were so progressive that they might have competed with his own projects.

Seen against this background, it is hardly surprising that the architectonic principles themselves caused less of a stir than the presentation of the design. Apart from ground plans and models, van Eesteren and van Doesburg also produced axonometric projections, and van Doesburg used these to draw counter-constructions. Published in *De Stijl* and *L'Architecture vivante*, an important architectural journal at the time, these works attracted a good deal of attention.[182]

These axonometric projections show each building either from above or below and in such a way that the rectangular ground plan appears diagonally within the picture plane, showing two sides at an oblique angle, though without the foreshortening of a central perspective. Unlike a conventional projection, several sides are shown simultaneously, with special emphasis on planes, lines and right angles.[183] In his counter-constructions van Doesburg took this division of building space even further.[184] He transferred van Eesteren's axonometric projections with tracing paper, but extracted only individual lines and then used the colours to change the building into an independent painting of horizontal and vertical planes. These counter-constructions, which preceded van Doesburg's paintings of 1924, were then called *Counter-Compositions* and continued his *De Stijl* paintings in the form of Elementarism.

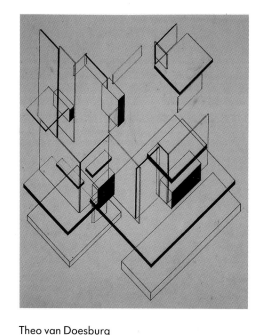

Theo van Doesburg

Counter-construction of the *Maison particulière*, 1923
Contra-constructie
Pencil and ink, 59.6 x 48 cm
Nederlands Documentatiecentrum voor de Bouwkunst, Amsterdam

Responses to the Rosenberg exhibition were rather mixed. Apart from several critical reactions, the exhibition was also influential; particularly van Eesteren and van Doesburg's projects. Le Corbusier was somewhat reserved towards *De Stijl*, for the Dutch architects were obviously entering an area he had regarded as his own domain. As early as 1915, his drafts for the so-called *Domino Houses* had shown the development of free floor plan design and a radical restriction of architectonic aids to no more than six ferroconcrete pillars and three slabs.[185] Also, in 1921, Le Corbusier had submitted exact plans for executing these ideas in his model series of *Citohan* houses.[186]

But there were important differences: Le Corbusier put far more emphasis on a skeletal style of building. A house was still a cubically self-contained unit. Nothing protruded into its surroundings, nor was the building split up into sections. In an article in his magazine *L'Esprit Nouveau*, he criticized *De Stijl* for having too many dogmatic restrictions to geometrical shapes, in particular rectangles, so that it could only ever allow a " ... stuttering and simplistic vocabulary of form".[187] However, Le Corbusier was profoundly impressed by the new possibilities offered by axonometric projections. In fact, the new architectural forms that had been brought forth by *De Stijl* ideals, such as the three Rosenberg projects, prompted him to change completely his plans for the *Villa La Roche*, his current building project.[188]

Theo van Doesburg

Counter-construction of the *Maison particulière*, 1923
Contra-constructie
Gouache on phototype, 57 x 57 cm
Rijksdienst Beeldende Kunst, The Hague

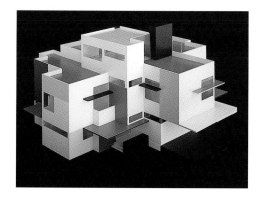
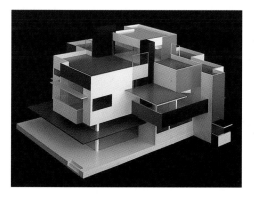

Theo van Doesburg and Cornelis van Eesteren

Model of the *Maison particulière*, 1923
Reconstruction of the maquette shown at the *De Stijl* exhibition at the *L'Effort moderne* gallery in Paris
Gemeentemuseum, The Hague

The model is shown from three different angles. The first one gives a view of the entrance, with the study to the right of the entrance, on the ground floor. The second view puts the functional section at the centre of attention – a narrow arrangement with three staggered levels containing cloakrooms, bathrooms, a toilet and a kitchen on the ground floor and two servants'

rooms next to a bedroom on the first floor. The third view shows the section adjacent to the functional parts with the protruding terrace in front of it and the big lounge stretching out behind it. The lounge is situated between a small study and the kitchen. Above it, on the top floor, are a bedroom and a guest room. All three views are, as it were, like a guided tour around the house, starting at the entrance and then proceeding clockwise. The strongly compartmentalized appearance of the building is further enhanced by its colour scheme. Sections that arbitrarily split up architectonic units exist side by side with sections that emphasize the various shapes.

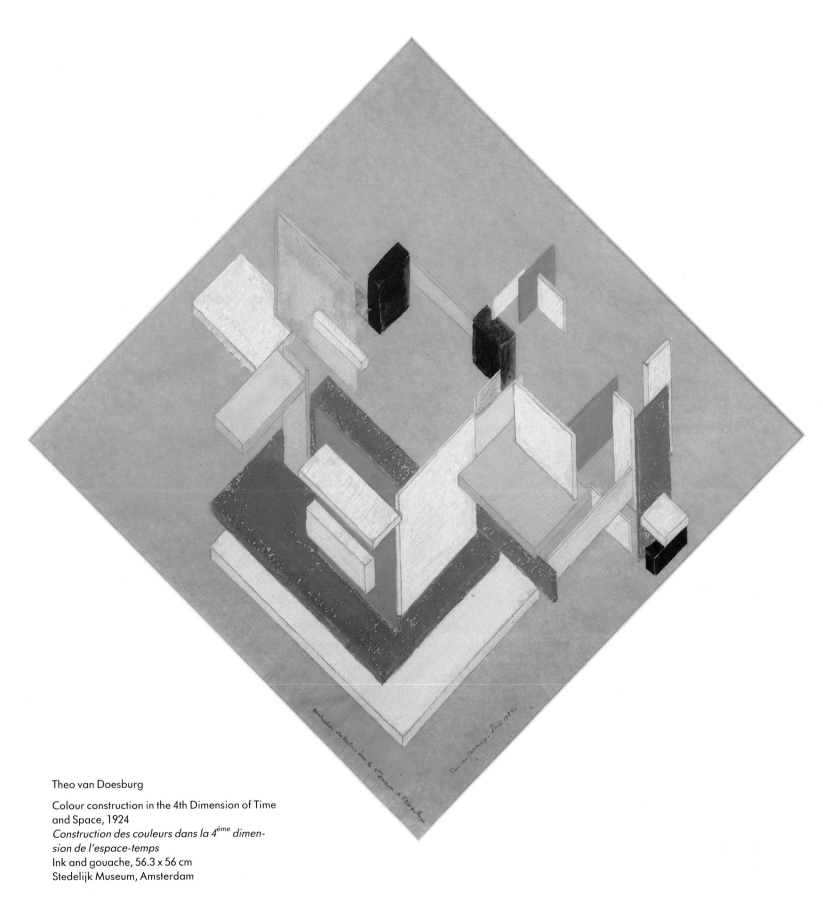

Theo van Doesburg

Colour construction in the 4th Dimension of Time
and Space, 1924
*Construction des couleurs dans la 4ème dimen-
sion de l'espace-temps*
Ink and gouache, 56.3 x 56 cm
Stedelijk Museum, Amsterdam

170

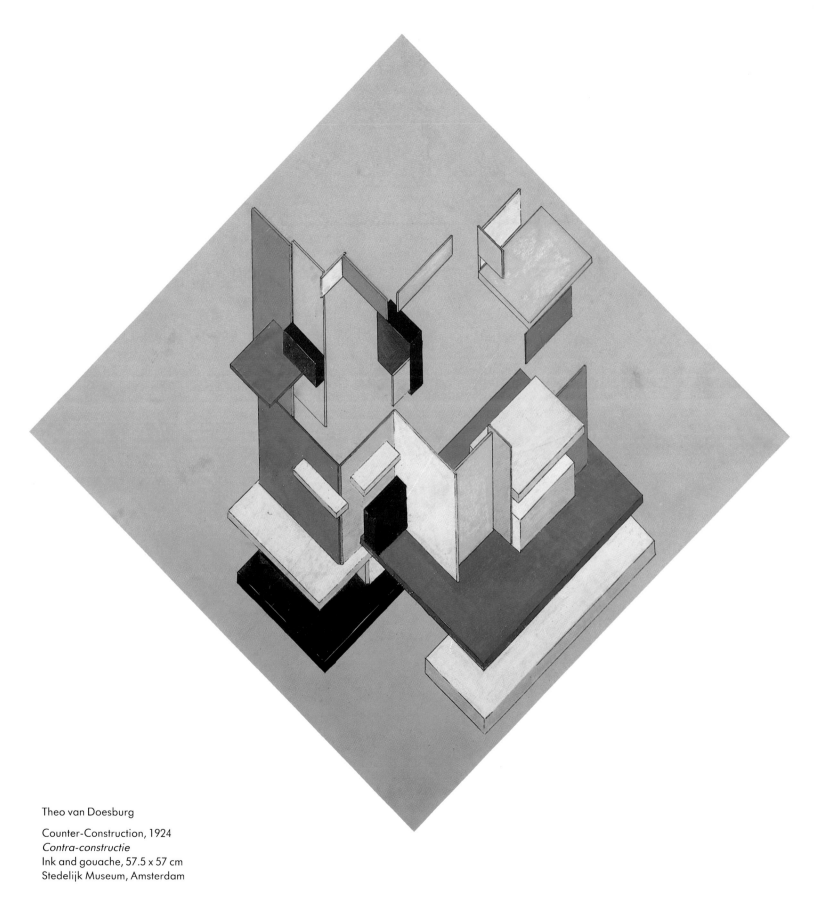

Theo van Doesburg

Counter-Construction, 1924
Contra-constructie
Ink and gouache, 57.5 x 57 cm
Stedelijk Museum, Amsterdam

Matters were somewhat different with the French architect Robert Mallet-Stevens.[189] When he was commissioned by the Viscount and Viscountess de Noailles to build a villa in Hyères, he invited van Doesburg to participate in the project and to build a conservatory for it (p. 174). The decisive impulse for this connection came from the clients who wanted to have their house designed as the sum of current avant-garde art. They also engaged Lipchitz, Laurens, Czaky and Brancusi for the sculptural design and later invited Man Ray to make a short film about the project (completed in 1928 as *Mystères du Château du Dé*).[190] Van Doesburg, incidentally, was the only painter involved in building the villa. He designed a scheme of colour planes that went beyond individual architectonic planes and in which the basic, dynamic elements were oblique lines.[191] Mallet-Stevens subsequently took over numerous architectonic forms from *De Stijl*, and this influence was apparent in two buildings in the Rue Mallet-Stevens, the *Maison Dreyfus* and the *Maison Martel*.[192]

De Stijl also had a noticeable influence on Gabriel Guévrékian (*Hôtel Relais Automobile*) and Pierre Chareau (*Maison de Verre*).[193] Mondrian's attitude to the Rosenberg exhibition was revealing.[194] He had already offered his help at the preliminary planning stage, but had his strong reservations about the restriction to purely architectural works. Although he praised the loose, open form of the three Eesteren/ Doesburg projects, he felt that the method of grouping rooms around a nucleus was too close to older, more conventional architectural methods, and he completely rejected the dynamic component. This attitude led to an argument with van Doesburg.

Mondrian's defection from *De Stijl* became inevitable in 1925 at the *Exposition des Arts Décoratifs* where *De Stijl* was not represented at all. Mondrian took this occasion to express himself positively about the architecture of a Dutch group called *Wendingen* (Changes), in whose context a conventional artist like Sybold van Ravesteyn was able to show furniture with *De Stijl* principles as purely decorative elements.[195] Also, Mondrian felt unable to follow Theo van Doesburg's "Elementarism," which had oblique lines to incorporate the idea of movement again as a fourth dimension.

However, this disaffection in 1925, when Mondrian finally turned his back on *De Stijl* for good, was a matter of theory and did not lead to a personal estrangement between the two protagonists. Nor was Mondrian totally indifferent towards questions of architectonic design. He even transformed his studio in Rue du Départ into a *De Stijl* room by painting large rectangular planes in primary colours and black, white and grey on his walls.[196]

Mondrian's aim was to achieve an interaction between the room and the paintings. He even had photographs of his studio made so that it would become known as an ideal exhibition room for *De Stijl* art (p. 177). To do so, he deliberately used a special photographic technique: following *De Stijl* ideals, all these photographs show a rectangular room which, due to its paintings and colour planes on the walls, has lost

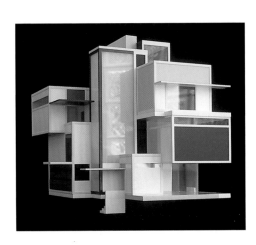

Theo van Doesburg's counter-construction of the Maison d'Artiste *can be compared here with a reconstruction of the model, shown at the* De Stijl *exhibition at the* L'Effort Moderne *gallery in Paris in 1923. The building is shown closed and also with a view to part of the central staircase inside. All three views show the entrance of the house. To the right of the entrance, on the ground floor and first floor, is the studio and, above it, on the second floor, a guest room protruding to the outside. On the left, behind the terrace, is the sitting room, situated between function rooms, and above it, on the first floor, another music room, also protruding to the outside. On the second floor is a recessed bedroom.*
Gemeentemuseum, The Hague

Theo van Doesburg

Counter-Construction of the *Maison d'Artiste*, 1923
Contra-constructie
Pencil, ink and gouache, 37 x 38 cm
Rijksdienst Beeldende Kunst, The Hague

its three-dimensional character. In reality, however, his studio was an irregular, pointed room with five corners and an old-fashioned round iron stove.

Mondrian's intensive study of space and dynamics during these years is also documented by his designs for stage sets and the interior designs for the Dresden art collector Ida Bienert (p. 175).

In February 1926, in Rome, the abstract painter and poet Michel Seuphor wrote a play called *L'Ephémère est éternel* (which, for financial reasons, was never performed). Mondrian designed a cubic stage set (p. 176) for this play, of which a replica was produced in 1964.[197]

Theo van Doesburg

Colour design of a conservatory for Viscount de
Noailles' villa, Hyères, 1924-1925
Kleurconstructie voor een bloemenkamertje
Pencil, ink and gouache, 54 x 61 cm
Stedelijk Van Abbe Museum, Eindhoven

Piet Mondrian

Draft for the *Salon de Mme. B . . ., à Dresden,*
1926
Illustration in the magazine *L'Art International*
d'Aujourd'hui VII, 1928, plate 50

These are designs for a room in Ida Bienert's
house in Plauen. Mondrian never actually went
there himself, which explains the mistake.

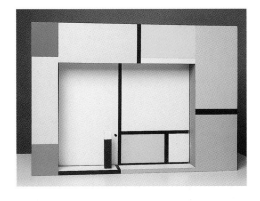

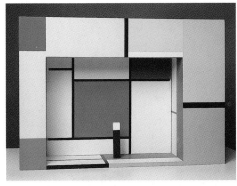

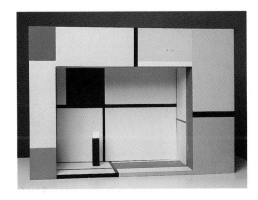

Piet Mondrian

Stage set models for Michel Seuphor's play in
three acts *L'Ephémère est éternel*, 1926
Reconstruction, cardboard and wood,
53.3 x 76.5 x 26.5 cm each
Stedelijk Van Abbe Museum, Eindhoven

For Ida Bienert's house in Plauen he designed a studio-like room that was never actually built at the time. Based on four of his drafts, the interior was reconstructed – or rather constructed for the first time – by the Pace Gallery in New York in 1970.[198] The room had to contain built-in beds and furniture in pre-defined places. Unlike Mondrian's paintings and stage designs, the room arrangement is made up entirely of colour planes with primary colours and three shades of grey. Lines do not function as autonomous compositional elements, so that the design is similar to Huszár's style.

Mondrian's room designs, for example those of his own studio, greatly influenced other artists and occasionally led to imitations, such as Jozef Peeters, Felix del Marle, Jean Gorin and César Domela.[199] Domela had met van Doesburg and Mondrian for the first time in 1924 and, under the influence of "Elementarism", had adopted an abstract style of painting with angular geometrical forms that were then tilted diagonally.

Domela designed his first studio flat on Kantstrasse in Berlin as a *De Stijl* interior, with straight, rectangular planes in primary colours as well as black, white and grey. In his second flat in Berlin he reduced this to a small number of grey planes because, he said, you cannot live in a painting with your family.[200]

Together with the German painter Vordemberge-Gildewart, Mondrian therefore functioned as a representative of "Elementarism" within *De Stijl*.[201] Both appeared in issue 75/76 (1926/27) of the magazine, where a manifesto on "Elementarism" was also published. The magazine contained some of their diagonal compositions which were compared with a Mondrian painting of 1922.

Those artists who had joined van Doesburg only recently included the designer Werner Graeff, Hans Richter (who published examples from an abstract animated film) and Karl Peter Röhl (who wanted to create a whole language out of abstract symbols and who was the inventor of pictograms).[202]

At the time, however, *De Stijl* was synonymous with Theo van Doesburg. The group itself had suffered a good deal of erosion and was faced with growing competition from similar art journals, of which the German magazine *G* has already been mentioned.[203] This explains van Doesburg's angry remark about *i 10*, which he described as a magazine whose content "consisted largely of things which I threw in the bin."[204] Launched in 1927, this Dutch art magazine contained contributions from nearly all former and current *De Stijl* artists. Theo van Doesburg himself, however, founded the Dadaist magazine *Mécano* as early as 1922, though it ceased publication in 1923.[205]

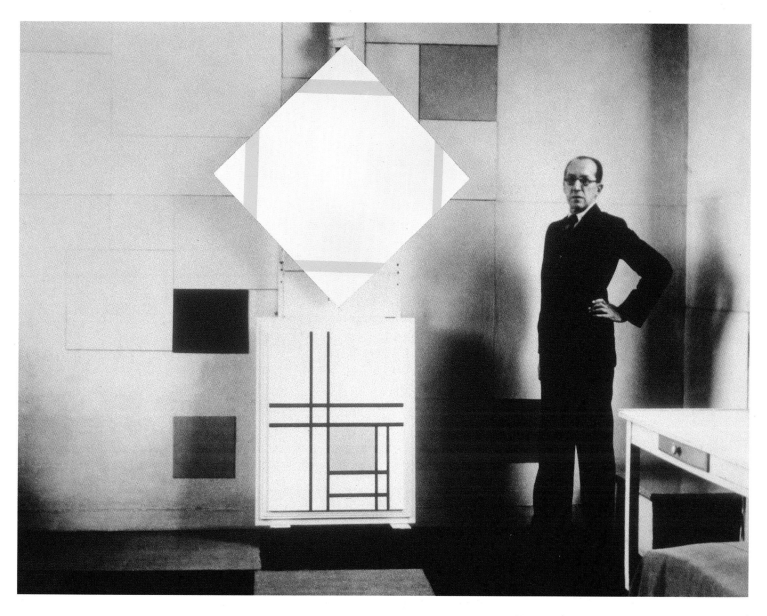

Vintage photograph of Mondrian's studio in Rue du Départ, Paris, c. 1926
Photomontage: Frank den Oudsten

Friedrich Vordemberge-Gildewart

Composition No. 31, 1927
Oil on canvas, 100 x 130 cm
Gemeentemuseum, The Hague

Friedrich Vordemberge-Gildewart

Composition No. 25, 1927
Oil on canvas, 80.2 x 60.4 cm
Staatsgalerie moderne Kunst, Munich

Theo van Doesburg's unbroken relationship with Dada and its artists eventually led to a large-scale project, the design for a restaurant/nightclub in Strasbourg, the so-called "Cabaret-Ciné-Bal", *Café Aubette*, on Place Kléber.[206]

It occupied the right wing of a building that was erected in the 18th century and whose façade was under preservation order. For several years the owners of the *Café Aubette*, the Horn brothers, had been trying to find a modern way of redecorating the building. Finally, they commissioned the Dadaist couple Jean Arp and Sophie Taeuber-Arp. The Arps, in turn, called in van Doesburg who immediately took charge of the project. He worked on the drafts from September 1926 to February 1928. As the *Café Aubette* had several floors and many different types of rooms, this was van Doesburg's first opportunity to realize his ideals on a larger scale. Although he admitted later that the *Café Aubette* had not been entirely successful (partly due to the economic restrictions on the use of materials), it can nevertheless be regarded as the most important contribution of *De Stijl* to everyday culture, along with the *Rietveld Schröder House*.

The interior that had to be redesigned included four floors with rooms for various entertainment and leisure purposes: a café, a bar, a dance hall with a cabaret in the basement, a pub, a restaurant, a tea room and dance halls that could also be used for film showings.

The three artists then divided up the work amongst themselves. Arp designed the floor of the hallway, the foyer bar and the dance hall (called *Caveau Dancing*, p. 181), as well as the colour scheme of the staircase. Taeuber-Arp designed the tearoom (pp. 181 and 182), the *Pâtisserie* and the bar next to the *Caveau Dancing*. Van Doesburg concentrated on the café-restaurant and brasserie on the ground floor and the large rooms on the first floor (though not for the foyer bar). The large ground-floor rooms (pp. 184 and 185) were dominated by the forms of van Doesburg's "Elementarism". The different dynamic arrangements on the other floors were summed up in the dynamism on the ground floor. On the other hand, due to the entertainment purpose of the building, it was geared towards a mobile public that would be walking through the passages from one room to another. As a result, functions were divided up and at the same time neutralized. This can be seen in van Doesburg's drafts for the two main halls on the first floor (pp. 186–193). Here he applied the dynamic diagonal construction principle of Elementarist *counter-compositions*. Walls and the one-sided, cubic purposes of the rooms were to be transcended, and even purely utilitarian elements, such as the rectangular film screen in the cinema room and the side staircase with the adjacent gallery, were to be disguised.

The colour planes were not simply painted on, but took the form of slightly raised plastic elements with interlocking bands that added depth and separated the different sections from one another. Van Doesburg also developed a system of lighting which combined both daylight and artificial illumination. The use of colour and light turned the rooms into purely abstract compositions.

Sophie Taeuber-Arp

Tearoom on the ground floor of the *Café Bal Aubette*, Strasbourg, 1928

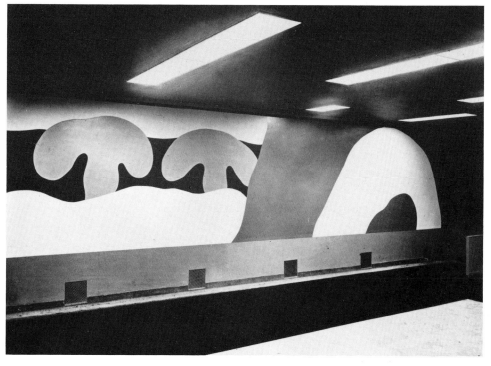

Jean Arp

Interior decoration of the *Caveau Dancing* in the basement of the *Café Bal Aubette*, Strasbourg, 1928

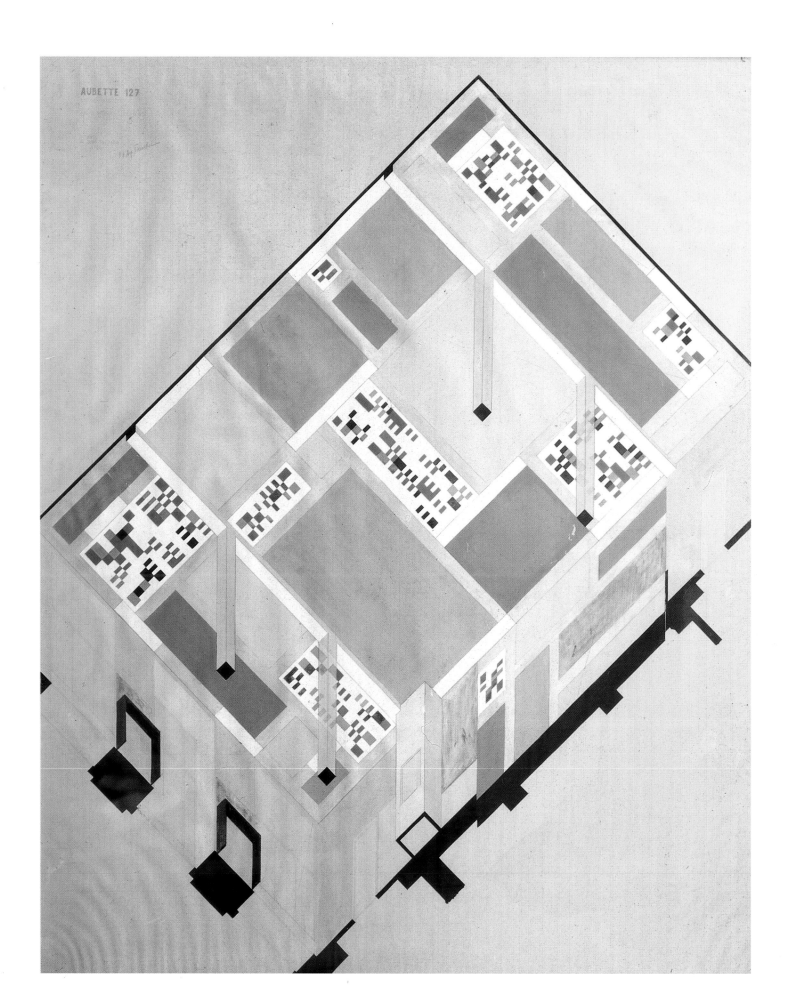

Wherever possible, natural material, such as wood, was of course avoided, and artificial material – concrete, iron, glass, etc. – was used instead. Van Doesburg also designed the furniture, which was then produced in series. He based it on models that seemed adequate enough with regard to form and function. The chairs, for example, were modelled on the Thonet pattern, though with changes in dimensions and proportions. This use of models was typical of the *Café Aubette* design: the mezzanine staircase is a variation on Oud's stairwell at the *De Vonk* holiday residence (p. 97). And the neutralization of walls in the café-restaurant and brasserie by means of mirrors that reflect their colour composition goes back to Adolf Loos' *American Bar* in Vienna.[207]

With his biomorphous wall paintings in the *Caveau Dancing*, Arp drew on Surrealist motifs, and Sophie Taeuber-Arp's small geometrical rectangles in the tearoom are reminiscent of paintings by Kandinsky.

The public totally rejected this form of decoration, and when the *Café Aubette* changed hands in 1938, the entire interior was completely redecorated by the new owners. Van Doesburg expressed himself very strongly about the lack of understanding among the public: "The public want to live in shit and so they'll have to die in shit."[208]

The design of the *Café Aubette* was complex but in the final analysis inconsistent because it was largely geared towards practical application. However, this was quite typical of *De Stijl*'s critical phase of international influence. At this stage it was even less of a unified movement than in its early phase. Instead, it provided a framework for a variety of different forms of design in painting and architecture, aimed at rational abstraction.

The problem of application had obviously turned out to be the acid test for the artists' ideals, and had often led to modifications of their views and the forms which they propagated in their manifestoes. It is therefore more appropriate to speak of an imitative, indirect effect on art, with an influence on details.

Sophie Taeuber-Arp

Draft for the tearoom on the ground floor of the *Café Aubette*
Projet pour le salon de thé
Gouache, pencil and ink, 123 x 99 cm
Musée d'Art Moderne, Strasbourg

Theo van Doesburg

Colour design for the ceiling of the café-
restaurant at the *Aubette*, 1927
*Kleurcompositie voor het plafond van het café-
restaurant*
Pencil, ink and gouache, 27.4 x 52.2 cm
Musée National d'Art Moderne, Paris

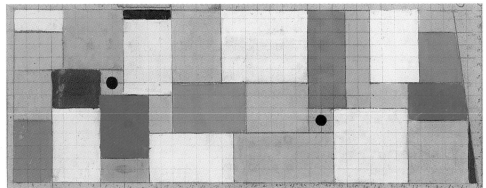

These photographs show two rooms situated on the ground floor of the Café Aubette – the café-restaurant, shortly before the furniture was added at the beginning of 1928 and the brasserie, complete with furniture. These are matched by Theo van Doesburg's definitive colour designs for the ceilings in each room. The simple long rectangular surfaces have been broken up into a complicated system of interlocking surfaces with primary and secondary colours as well as black, white and grey. The design of the walls corresponds to this, so that the structure of the rooms is covered up by the arbitrary decomposition of the architectural environment.

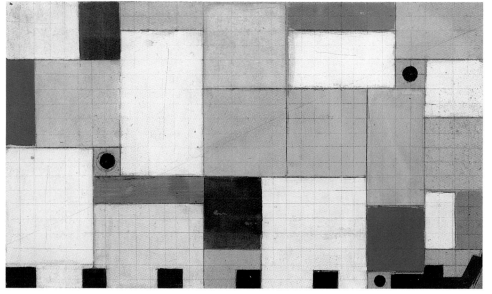

Theo van Doesburg

Colour design of the ceiling at the café-brasserie
of the *Café Aubette*, 1927
*Kleucompositie voor het plafond van de café-
brasserie*
Pencil, ink and gouache, 23.8 x 37.6 cm
Musée National d'Art Moderne, Paris

Theo van Doesburg

Colour design for the wall of the cinema-dance
hall, adjacent to the bar, 1927
*Kleucompositie voor de grote feestzaal, wand
aan de kant van de bar*
Pencil, ink, silver paint and gouache on phototype, 44.5 x 89 cm
Rijksdienst Beeldende Kunst, The Hague

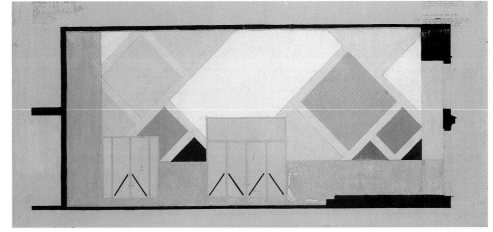

Theo van Doesburg

Colour design for the ceiling of the cinema-dance hall, 1927
Kleurcompositie voor het plafond van de grote feestzaal
Pencil, ink, gouache and silver paint,
110 x 72.5 cm
Rijksdienst Beeldende Kunst, The Hague

This photograph, taken at the beginning of 1928, shows a view of the cinema-dance hall on the first floor of the Café Aubette, looking towards the entrance. The hall was used as a ballroom and for showing films. The two paintings are drafts for the colour design of the entrance wall and the ceiling. They give some idea of the visual impact of the room which now no longer exists. Note, however, that van Doesburg misunderstood the projection ratios, and the colour draft for the ceiling is therefore laterally inverted. The overall effect must be seen as less expressive than the photograph might suggest, bearing in mind that the latter misrepresents the shades. This is because the juxtaposed planes with primary and secondary colours, as well as black, white and grey, have a variety of different spatial values. On the other hand, the far-reaching decomposition of the spatial structure, originally marked by right angles, was intended and also achieved. Unlike the design of the restaurant rooms on the ground floor and unlike the small dance hall on the same floor, van Doesburg here applies the diagonal arrangement of his Elementarist counter-compositions (cf. also illus. p. 77), so that the room becomes dynamic. The overall effect is further enhanced by counteracting any possible overlapping of colours. This is achieved by inserting raised bands 13 in. (35 cm) wide and 1 in. (4 cm) high, between the sections. This dynamic design also takes account of the different functions of the room, which are also characterized by movement.

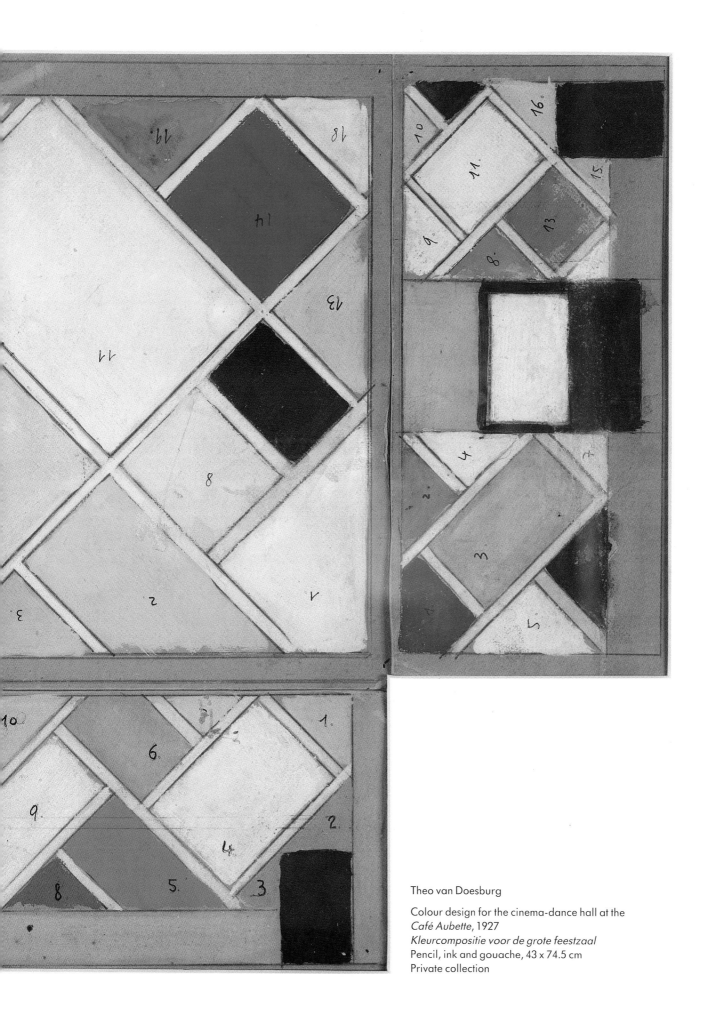

Theo van Doesburg

Colour design for the cinema-dance hall at the
Café Aubette, 1927
Kleurcompositie voor de grote feestzaal
Pencil, ink and gouache, 43 x 74.5 cm
Private collection

189

This photograph, taken in 1928, shows the cinema-dance hall of the Café Aubette from an oblique angle, looking towards the film projection wall and above all overlooking the gallery wall opposite the side of the window. Both the narrow wall above the entrance and the gallery wall had planes built into them which actually disrupted van Doesburg's anti-architectonic spatial composition. These were consistently covered up by diagonal arrangements, and their effect is still apparent from the drafts.

The floor and the side of the windows, on the other hand, had colour planes with straight verticals and horizontals. This means that the room was dominated by two different principles of composition.

Theo van Doesburg

Colour design for the wall opposite the Place Kléber in the cinema-dance hall at the *Café Aubette*, 1927
Kleurcompositie voor de grote feestzaal, wand tegenover de Place Kléber
Ink, silver paint and gouache on phototype, 46 x 105 cm
Rijksdienst Beeldende Kunst, The Hague

Theo van Doesburg

Colour design for the film projection wall of the cinema-dance hall at the *Café Aubette*, 1927
Kleurcompositie voor de grote feestzaal, wand met vlak voor filmprojectie
Ink, silver paint and gouache on phototype, 45 x 94 cm
Rijksdienst Beeldende Kunst, The Hague

Theo van Doesburg

Colour design for the ceiling of the small dance hall at the *Café Aubette*, 1927
Kleurcompositie voor het plafond van de kleine feestzaal
Pencil, crayon and gouache on phototype, 72.5 x 109 cm
Rijksdienst Beeldende Kunst, The Hague

These two photographs, taken in 1928, give a view of the small dance hall designed by Theo van Doesburg.
The photographs of the building, which no longer exists, are matched by Theo van Doesburg's drafts for the ceiling and the narrow, windowless side of the room, giving some idea of the effect of the interior (bearing in mind, however, that van Doesburg's projection was faulty, as it showed the ceiling laterally inverted.)

Theo van Doesburg

Colour design for the wall opposite the Place Kléber in the small dance hall at the *Café Aubette*, 1927
Kleurcompositie voor de wand tegenover de Place Kléber in de kleine feestzaal
Ink, crayon and gouache on phototype, 45 x 80 cm
Rijksdienst Beeldende Kunst, The Hague

Although the sections of the wall and ceiling are arranged more statically and strictly than in the cinema-dance hall, they nevertheless create a similarly dynamic impression. The room combines the different form principles from the other rooms that were designed by Theo van Doesburg, so that the cinema-dance hall – as the last of the first-floor rooms – is a synthesis of the artist's interior design at the Café Aubette.

Jacobus Johannes Pieter Oud

Terraced houses at the Weissenhof Estate,
seen from the gardens
Stuttgart, 1927

Jacobus Johannes Pieter Oud

Terraced houses at the Weissenhof Estate,
seen from the street
Stuttgart, 1927

The influence of *De Stijl* became apparent when Oud made his contribution to the Weissenhof Estate, the International Architectural Exposition in Stuttgart in 1927, alongside other internationally renowned architects such as Le Corbusier and Mies van der Rohe.[209] The functionalist orientation of the exposition programme was very convenient for Oud, because he had already been able to apply the new vocabulary of form to inexpensive, rational houses at the Hook of Holland and Kiefhoek. The idea of building houses at a minimum of cost and space was therefore a familiar task to him.

The use of form in his five terraced houses at the Weissenhof Estate is convincing because it is both clear and economical. They are composed of a small number of cubic elements, so that the street and garden fronts are in a clear, though functionally unrelated, contrast with each other. Unlike previous Dutch houses of this kind, their cubic block-like extensions on the side of the street are reserved for purely functional rooms (laundry room, drying room), and those parts of the building that are based on rectangles include sitting rooms, bedrooms and kitchens. Taken together and placed in a row, both fronts form a rhythmic wave of alternating open and closed forms.[210]

In the mid-Twenties this utilization and functional application of *De Stijl*'s architectonic vocabulary of form was still opposed quite vehemently by van Doesburg, though he, too, was affected by it. Starting in 1929 the artist designed a house for himself and his wife in Meudon, using his own drafts.[211] It was built in 1930 (p. 196) and shows all the features of a calmer style, and a noticeable transformation of the *De Stijl* principle. Instead of protruding freely into the surrounding space, it is more functional and architecturally self-contained.

On the whole, van Doesburg had developed a style with this building which combined *De Stijl* principles with criteria of usefulness, though without entirely rejecting the basic dialectical notions of *De Stijl* architecture. It was both simple and ingenious and had reached a stage that was now also characteristic of International Style, so that van Doesburg's building can be compared with the terraced houses of Oud, Rietveld and even Le Corbusier.

The erosion of *De Stijl* had now become obvious. It had started at the beginning of the Twenties, with the dissolution of the core group, and continued with the individual projects of the different artists, including those who had only just joined the movement. *De Stijl* had become absorbed by a style which united elements of Constructivism, *Bauhaus* and other, similar groups in Europe – movements that varied widely but were held together by a common vocabulary of form.

Gerrit Rietveld

Zaudy's shop in Wesel, 1928
This vintage photograph shows the front windows of a shop (destroyed since then) in Wesel, a German town on the Lower Rhine. It was one of Rietveld's few works outside the Netherlands.

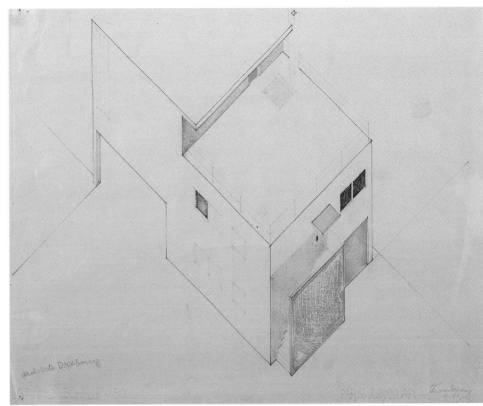

Theo van Doesburg

Studio and residential house in Meudon-Val-Fleury, 29, Rue Charles-Infroit

Exterior view, photograph taken during construction, which was started in 1930

Van Doesburg's studio/residence in Meudon was built as a simple long rectangle and in the form of two cubic blocks, shifted vertically out of place against each other. An open form and a closed form were set diagonally against one another. The exterior division into two parts agrees with the functional distribution of space: on the ground floor an open terrace is matched by a closed cube which contains purely utilitarian rooms, such as a garage and a kitchen, while the studio, which extends over two of the top floors, contrasts with the single-storey living area (bedrooms, library, music room and bathroom), of which an open terrace affords a view.

Axonometric projection with colour draft for the studio and residential house in Meudon, 1929–1930
Axonometrie met kleurstudie
Pencil and coloured pencil on phototype, 59 x 55 cm
Rijksdienst Beeldende Kunst, The Hague

Axonometric projection, seen from four different sides
Studio and residential house in Meudon, 1929–1930
Projectie over elkaar van vier axonometrieë van vier verschillende kanten
Pencil and ink, 69.7 x 53.2 cm
Nederlands Documentatiecentrum voor de Bouwkunst, Amsterdam

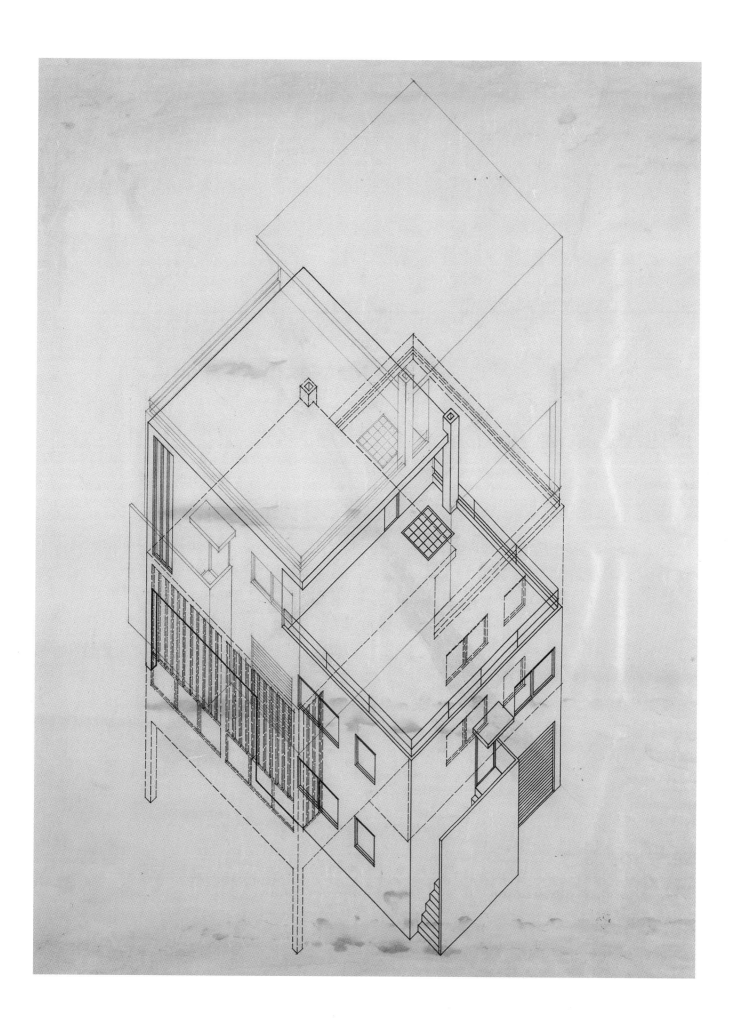

Notes

1 In: *De Stijl* No. 79–84, 1927, p. 4, special edition for the tenth anniversary. German translation in Jaffé (see note 4), p. 37.

2 Reyner Banham, *The Revolution of Architecture*, London 1960: chapters 12 and 14 are about *De Stijl*.

3 Although the last issue of the magazine *De Stijl* was published in January 1932, this was really a commemorative booklet in honour of Theo van Doesburg, who had died in March 1931. The last regular issue was published in 1928. As van Doesburg was the editor-in-chief of *De Stijl*, his death is generally regarded as the end of the *De Stijl* movement.

4 This was in fact the subtitle of a monograph by Hans L.C. Jaffé (ed.), *De Stijl 1917–1931, The Dutch Contribution to Modern Art*, Amsterdam 1956, a book that became fundamental to the international discussion on the question of *De Stijl*.

5 Henry Russel Hitchcock, Jr., and Philip Johnson, *The International Style: Architecture since 1922*, New York 1932 (revised edition 1966). This publication, which was fundamental to the concept and evaluation of International Style, names Oud as the only Dutchman.

6 The most important publications in this context are Carel Blotkamp (ed.), *De Stijl 1917–1922. The Formative Years*, Cambridge/Mass. and London 1986 (original Dutch edition 1982); Evert van Straaten (ed.), *Theo van Doesburg 1883–1931. Een documentaire op basis van materiaal uit de schenking Van Moorsel*, 's-Gravenhage 1983; Sjarel Ex and Els Hoek, *Vilmos Huszár, schilder en ontwerper 1884–1960. De grote onbekende van De Stijl*, Utrecht 1985; Evert van Straaten, *Theo van Doesburg, schilder en architect*, 's-Gravenhage 1988; *Rietveld Schröder Archief*, ed. by Centraal Museum Utrecht, Utrecht 1988.

7 Examples of complemented constructions of Mondrian's lozenges can be found in E.A. Carmean, Jr., *Mondrian. The Diamond Compositions*, Washington 1979.

8 Clara Weyergraf, *Piet Mondrian und Theo van Doesburg. Deutung von Werk und Theorie*, Munich 1979, pp. 8ff. Discussing the contrast between the simultaneousness of composition and subsequent reflexion, a contrast that is present in all these paintings, Clara Weyergraf tries to interpret this as a typical feature of Mondrian's view of art.

9 Els Hoek in Blotkamp (see note 6), pp. 62-69, gives an analysis par excellence of the compositional mechanisms in the positive/ negative treatment of the centre and periphery in Mondrian's art of the early Twenties.

10 Cf. R.W. D. Oxenaar, *Bart van der Leck tot 1920. Een primitief van de nieuwe tijd*, doctoral thesis, Utrecht 1976, especially pp. 141ff.

11 Ingrid Riedel, *Farben in Religion, Gesellschaft, Kunst und Psychotherapie*, Stuttgart/Berlin 1983; Walter Hess, *Das Problem der Farbe in den Selbstzeugnissen der Maler von Cézanne bis Mondrian*, Mittenwald 1981; Lorenz Dittmann, *Farbgestaltung und Farbtheorie in der abendländischen Malerei*, Darmstadt 1987; *Rot Gelb Blau. Die Primärfarben in der Kunst des 20. Jahrhunderts*, exhibition catalogue, Kassel 1988.

12 An analysis of the "universal language" of modern art can be found in Steven A. Mansbach, *Visions of Totality. László Moholy-Nagy, Theo van Doesburg and El Lissitzky*, Ann Arbor 1980, pp. 87ff., though the book unfortunately only contains theoretical statements of the artists.

13 Michel Seuphor, *Piet Mondrian. Leben und Werk*, Cologne 1957, esp. pp. 43-150; L.J.F. Wijsenbeek, *Piet Mondrian*, Recklinghausen 1968, pp. 9-95; for a general survey cf. Maria Grazia Ottolenghi, *L'opera completa di Mondrian*, Milan 1974; Frank Elgar, *Mondrian*, London 1968.

14 Robert P. Welsh, *Piet Mondrian's Early Career. The "naturalistic" periods*, New York/London 1977 (doctoral thesis, Princeton 1965); cf. in general: *Kunstenaren der idee. Symbolistische tendensen in Nederland, ca. 1880–1930*, exhibition catalogue, 's-Gravenhage 1978.

15 Seuphor (see note 13), pp. 82 f.; Wijsenbeek (see note 13), pp. 71f.; Els Hoek in: Blotkamp (see note 6), pp. 40ff.

16 His theory was published in *De Stijl*, issues 1/1917, 2/1917, 4/1918 (recte: 3/1918), 4/ 1918, 5/1918, 7/1918, 8/1918, 9/1918, 10/ 1918, 11/1918, 12/1918.

17 Seuphor (see note 13), pp. 72 f.; Wijsenbeek (see note 13), pp. 30ff.

18 For a general survey cf. Pierre Daix, *Der Kubismus in Wort und Bild*, Stuttgart 1982.

19 Piet Mondrian, *Plastic Art and Pure Plastic Art 1937 and Other Essays, 1941–1943*, New York 1951 (3rd edition), p. 10. The quotation was taken from his essay "Toward the True Vision of Reality", p. 54.

20 This quotation is taken from the same essay as the one in note 19 (see note 19, p. 10).

21 Els Hoek in: Blotkamp (see note 6), pp. 50ff. and Cees Hillhorst in: Blotkamp (see note 6), pp. 160ff.; Oxenaar (see note 10), pp. 106ff.

22 Van Doesburg and Huszár had been invited by Van der Leck to look at his latest works at Mrs. Kröller-Müller's house in The Hague, which they did between Christmas and New Year's Day, 1916. On New Year's Eve van Doesburg wrote an enthusiastic letter to van der Leck, telling him that he wanted to write a book about his works and emphasizing particularly the Triptych. Blotkamp in Blotkamp (see note 6), p. 12.

23 *Bart van der Leck, 1876–1958*, exhibition catalogue, Otterlo/Amsterdam 1976; Bart

van der Leck, *1876–1958. A la recherche de l'image des temps modernes*, exhibition catalogue, Institut Néerlandais, Paris 1980. Both catalogues give comprehensive documentations of the genesis of van der Leck's "abstract" compositions.

24 Hans L.C. Jaffé, *Mondrian und De Stijl*, Cologne 1967, illus. 19.

25 Van der Leck Catalogue 1976 (see note 23) and Van der Leck Catalogue 1980 (see note 23); Oxenaar (see note 10). For a stylistic analysis that attempts to identify all the possible inspirations (Egyptian art, the works of Paolo Ucello, etc.) in W.C. Feltkamp, *B.A. van der Leck, Leven en werken*, Leiden 1956. On van der Leck's clients cf. S. van Deventer, *Kröller-Müller: De geschiedenis van een cultureel levenswerk*, Haarlem 1956.

26 Ingo F. Walther/Rainer Metzger, *Vincent van Gogh*, 2 vols., Cologne 1989, vol. 2.

27 Van der Leck Catalogue 1976 (see note 23), no page number, Van der Leck Catalogue 1980 (see note 23), no. 42.

28 angela thomas, *denkbilder, materialien zur entwicklung von georges vantongerloo*, Düsseldorf 1987, pp. 12ff.; *Georges Vantongerloo. A Traveling Retrospective Exhibition*, Brussels 1980, pp. 16-20; Nicolette Gast in: Blotkamp (see note 6), pp. 231ff.

29 thomas (see note 28), pp. 22ff.; Gast (see note 28), p. 232. On the person and oeuvre of Schmalzigaug, who has only been rediscovered very recently, see Pontus Hulten (ed.), *Futurismo & Futurismi*, exhibition catalogue, Venice/Milan 1986, pp. 261, 262 and 566.

30 For a general survey cf. Hulten (see note 29) and Maurizio Calvesi, *Futurismus*, Cologne 1987.

31 Joost Baljeu, *Theo van Doesburg*, London/ New York 1974, pp. 13-19; Hannah L. Hedrick, *Theo van Doesburg, Propagandist and Practitioner of the Avant-Garde, 1909–1923*, Ann Arbor 1980, pp. 1-82; Blotkamp (see note 22), pp. 4ff.

32 Blotkamp (see note 22), pp. 8-10, van Straaten 1983 (see note 6), pp. 42-45 and illus. pp. 60 and 61.

33 Blotkamp (see note 22), op.cit.

34 Blotkamp (see note 22), p. 11; Sjarel Ex in: Blotkamp (see note 6), pp. 78ff.; Sjarel Ex and Els Hoek, *Vilmos Huszár, schilder en ontwerper 1884–1960* (see note 6), pp. 29ff.

35 Blotkamp (see note 31), pp. 11ff.; van Straaten 1983 (see note 6), pp. 67ff.; van Straaten 1988 (see note 6), pp. 24ff.

36 Quoted from Blotkamp (note 22), p. 14

37 Blotkamp (see note 22), pp. 16-18; van Straaten 1983 (see note 6), p. 68, van Straaten 1988 (see note 6), pp. 28ff.

38 Huszár's stained glass compositions of this period – especially the ones for the Bruynzeel's Villa *De Arendshoeve*–are identical and composed asymmetrically. Ex/Hoek

(see note 6), pp. 29ff.; Ex in: Blotkamp (see note 6), pp. 86ff.

39 Kirk Varnedoe, *Wien 1900. Kunst. Architektur & Design*, Cologne 1987; Klaus-Jürgen Sembach, Gabriele Leuthäuser and Peter Gössel, *Möbeldesign des 20. Jahrhunderts*, Cologne, undated (1988) pp. 55 ff; Gottfried Fliedl, *Gustav Klimt*, Cologne 1990 (English edition), pp. 144-153. Especially *Palais Stoclet*, which was designed and built by the Viennese Secessionists, greatly influenced the history of art and design in the Benelux countries. Cf. also notes 121 and 124.

40 In a retrospective article for the *Neue Schweizer Rundschau*, 1929, pp. 43f., Theo van Doesburg wrote, "We wanted to replace the brown world by a white one. These two colour concepts summed up the whole essential difference between the old and the new. The brown world, which pushes against the outer limits of Cubism, expresses itself in a lyrical, hazy and sentimental vein. The white world started with Cézanne and led to elementary construction, via van Gogh and the heyday of Cubism …" Quoted in Jaffé (see note 4), p. 23.

41 Van Straaten 1983 (see note 6), pp. 112-114; van Straaten 1988 (see note 6), pp. 84ff.; I am indebted to Wouter van der Horst, Drachten, for this suggestion.

42 The depiction of agricultural activities to illustrate the four seasons or the months of the year can be found in cathedrals, in book illustrations, etc. *Lexikon der christlichen Ikonographie*, volume 3, 1971, columns 274-279, especially pp. 277ff.

43 On the coining of terms see Ernst H. Gombrich, *Aby Warburg, An Intellectual Biography*, London 1970, pp. 179ff. and passim.

44 Klaus Lankheit, *Das Triptychon als Pathosformel*, Heidelberg 1959; more narrowly, in the context of *De Stijl*: Carel Blotkamp, "Triptieken in Stijl" in Carel Blotkamp, *Mondriaan in detail*, Utrecht/Antwerp 1987, pp. 102-122.

45 Vantongerloo did indeed derive his inspiration from altarpieces – works from the circle around Rogier van der Weydens. Gast (see note 28), pp. 252cs. Gast (see note 28), pp. 252f.; Blotkamp (see note 44), pp. 120f.; thomas (see note 28), pp. 164ff.

46 Trevor Fawcett and Clive Philpot (eds.), *The Art Press. Two Centuries of Art Magazines*, London 1976, esp. pp. 23-39 and 41ff. (on *De Stijl* and other comparable magazines).

47 Hulten (see note 29), pp. 16ff. and 512ff.

48 *De Stijl* No. 2, 1917, p. 13. German translation in Jaffé, *Mondrian* (see note 24), p. 41.

49 Rudolf Heinz, *Stil als geisteswissenschaftliche Kategorie. Problemgeschichtliche Untersuchungen zum Stilbegriff im 19. und 20. Jahrhundert*, Würzburg 1986, pp. 11ff. and 267ff.

50 *Gottfried Semper und die Mitte des 19. Jahrhunderts*, Basle/Stuttgart 1976, pp. 68ff. (for

the concept of *style* in Semper's book on this subject) and pp. 308ff. (for the influence of Semper on Berlage).

51 On the position of *De Stijl* in history and the history of art in general see Jaffé (see note 4), pp. 49-99; on the name of the magazine op.cit. p. 154 and Mildred Friedman (ed.), *Visions of Utopia. De Stijl: 1917–1931*, 2nd edition, Oxford 1986, p. 25. Van Doesburg had originally planned to call his journal *The Straight Line*.

52 For a general survey see Maurice Tuchman and Judi Freeman (ed.), *The Spiritual in Art: Abstract Painting 1890–1985*, New York 1986.

53 Willy Rotzler, *Konstruktive Konzepte. Eine Geschichte der konstruktiven Kunst vom Kubismus bis heute*, Zurich 1977.

54 *De Stijl* No. 9, 1918, p. 103; Mondrian is quoting, as he himself states, from the article "Reine Vernunft" by Bolland. A quotation can also be found in the German translation of the article, Jaffé (see note 24), p. 67.

55 Jaffé (see note 4), pp. 135ff.

56 *De Stijl* No. 1, p. 4. German translation in Jaffé (see note 24), p. 36.

57 Jaffé (see note 4), pp. 74ff.

58 Siegfried Giedion, *Mechanization Takes Command*, Oxford 1948

59 Jaffé (see note 4), pp. 109ff.

60 For a general survey of the philosophical and theosophical, etc. sources that influenced the artists see Jaffé (see note 4), pp. 65ff. In particular, Schoenmaeker's writings (especially *Het nieuwe wereldbeeld*, published in 1915) had a considerable influence on Theo van Doesburg and Piet Mondrian. Many of Mondrian's concepts and phrases were direct borrowings from Schoenmaeker, and his axiomatic way of arguing and his central concepts match the thinking and theories of theosophists. G. von Purucker, *Theosophisches Wörterbuch*, Stuttgart 1949 (The link was very kindly pointed out by Friederike Schmidt-Neben, Göttingen). – On the significance of the supposed or actual influence of Spinoza's writings on *De Stijl*, see Jaffé, op. cit. pp. 96f.; thomas (see note 28), pp. 26ff.; Beat Wismer, *Mondrians ästhetische Utopie*, Baden 1985, especially pp. 36ff.'

61 Apart from Jaffé (see notes 4 and 24), cf. also Mondrian (see note 19), Seuphor (see note 13), *De Stijl* No. 1–89, Sergio Polano (ed.), Theo van Doesburg, *Scritti di arte e di architettura*, Rome 1979 (with the best bibliography on van Doesburg's writings).

62 Cees Hillhorst in: Blotkamp (see note 6), pp. 178f.

63 *De Stijl* No. 1, 1917, p. 1.

64 Els Hoek in: Blotkamp (see note 6), p. 54.

65 Seuphor (see note 13), p. 162; Friedman (see note 51), pp. 80ff.

66 Cf. Seuphor (see note 13), No. 305; Ottolen-

ghi (see note 13), No. 318; *Mondrian und de Stijl*, exhibition catalogue of the Gmurzynska Gallery, Cologne 1979, p. 181.

67 Jaffé (see note 4), p. 22; Els Hoek in: Blotkamp (see note 6), pp. 54f. (letter dated 13 February 1917).

68 R.P. Welsh in: Friedman (see note 51), pp. 31f. and Joop Joosten in: Friedman (see note 51), pp. 60f.; Robert P. Welsh in: F. Bulhof (ed.), *De Stijl. Modernism in the Netherlands and Belgium in the First Quarter of the 20th Century*, The Hague 1976, pp. 76ff.; Els Hoek in: Blotkamp (see note 6), pp. 55ff.; Sjarel Ex in: Blotkamp (see note 6), pp. 90ff.

69 Els Hoek in: Blotkamp (see note 6), pp. 59ff.; Carel Blotkamp in: Blotkamp (see note 44), pp. 123ff.

70 Cf. Seuphor (see note 13), p. 37; Wijsenbeek (see note 13), p. 142.

71 *Mondrian. Zeichnungen, Aquarelle, New Yorker Bilder*, exhibition catalogue, Stuttgart 1980, pp. 192-194, nos. 106-109.

72 *De Stijl* 7, Nos. 75/76, pp. 37f.

73 Mondrian (see note 19), p. 14.

74 Jaffé (see note 4), p. 178; the letter was dated 23 January 1930.

75 Cf. van Straaten 1988 (see note 6), p. 246, illus. 299 in conjunction with p. 247, illus. 300; Baljeu (see note 31), p. 40.

76 Georges Vantongerloo, *L'art et son Avenir*, p. 26; quoted by Jaffé (see note 4), p. 130.

77 For a general survey of this point see Jaffé (see note 4), pp. 130f. On Spinoza's influence cf. note 60. This view, too, must be seen as based on Schoenmaeker, who wrote an essay in 1916 on the "Principles of Formative Mathematics (*Beginselen der beeldende wiskunde*, Bussum 1916); Wismer (see note 60), p. 51.

78 Nicolette Gast (see note 28), p. 254.

79 Gast (see note 28), pp. 248f.; thomas (see note 28), pp. 132ff.

80 thomas (see note 28), pp. 99ff.; Gast (see note 28), p. 240.

81 Gast (see note 28), pp. 240ff.; thomas (see note 28), pp. 78ff.

82 Cf. the list of works in the 1980 Vantongerloo Catalogue (see note 28).

83 Christian Zervos, *Domela*, Amsterdam 1966, pp. 7ff., illus. 5ff.

84 Ger Hamsen in: Friedman (see note 51), pp. 45ff.; for a general survey of this subject cf. Jaffé (see note 4), pp. 85ff. and 135ff.

85 In his essay "anti-tendenskunst" in *De Stijl* 6, No. 2, 1923, p. 18.

86 See note 85, p. 17.

87 K. Schippers, *Holland Dada*, Amsterdam 1974, pp. 30-41, especially p. 32.

88 Giovanni Fanelli, *De Stijl*, Rome/Bari 1983; Hans Oud, *J.J.P. Oud Architekt 1890–1963*, 's-Gravenhage 1984, pp. 28ff.; Günther Stamm, *J.J.P. Oud, Bauten und Projekte 1906 bis 1963*, Mainz/Berlin 1984, pp. 35ff.

89 For a general discussion see Otto Antonia Graf, *Die Kunst des Quadrats. Zum Werk von Frank Lloyd Wright*, 2 vols., Vienna/Cologne/Graz 1983. On Wright's influence on *De Stijl* cf. Fanelli (see note 88), *Het Nieuwe Bouwen. De Nieuwe Beelding in de architectuur. De Stijl*, Delft/The Hague 1983, pp. 17ff. and passim.

90 Fanelli (see note 88), pp. 27ff. and 113-118; Friedman (see note 51), p. 100; Eveline Vermeulen in: Blotkamp (see note 6), pp. 212ff.; for a general survey: *robert van 't hoff tentoonstelling*, Eindhoven 1967.

91 In: *De Stijl* 2, No. 3, 1919, pp. 27-31.

92 This and the following discussions can be found in Fanelli (see note 88), pp. 113ff.

93 Fanelli (see note 88), passim.

94 In *De Stijl* 1, 1917, pp. 6f.

95 Fanelli (s. note 88), pp. 14ff.; H. Esser in: Blotkamp (s. note 6), pp. 127f.; Oud (s. note 88), pp. 38f.; Stamm (s. note 88), pp. 40f.; van Straaten 1988 (s. note 6), pp. 28ff.

96 Fanelli (see note 88), p. 14; van Straaten 1988 (see note 6), p. 30; Blotkamp (see note 22), pp. 14f. (pointing out that there is, in fact, a difference between the aesthetic idea and the motif, as the motif in *Composition II* is a seated figure); Nancy J. Troy, *The De Stijl Environment*, Cambridge/Mass. and London 1983, pp. 24f.

97 Fanelli (see note 88), pp. 13f.; Friedman (see note 51), p. 101; Oud (see note 88), pp. 39ff.; Stamm (see note 88), pp. 41ff., van Straaten 1988 (see note 6), pp. 48ff.; Esser in: Blotkamp (see note 6), pp. 130ff.; Troy (see note 96), pp. 17ff.

98 Cf. van Straaten 1988 (see note 6), p. 24-59.

99 Van Straaten 1988 (see note 6), pp. 36-47; Blotkamp (see note 22), pp.16ff.; Troy (see note 96), pp. 25ff.

100 Van Straaten 1988 (see note 6), pp. 56ff.

101 Ezio Godoli, *Jan Wils, Frank Lloyd Wright e De Stijl*, Calenzano 1980, pp. 28ff.; Fanelli (see note 88), pp. 20f. and pp. 119-122 (our analysis follows this discussion); Sjarel Ex and Els Hoek in: Blotkamp (see note 6), pp. 190ff.

102 *De Stijl* 2, No. 5, 1919, pp. 58ff.

103 Fanelli (see note 88), pp. 33f.; Oud (see note 88), pp. 60ff.; Stamm (see note 88), pp. 57ff.; Esser (see note 95), pp. 133ff.

104 According to Stamm (see note 88), pp. 58ff.

105 Stamm (see note 88), p. 59 and illus. 40; Oud (see note 88), pp. 64f.; Marijke Küper in Blotkamp (see note 6), p. 267 and illus. 254.

106 Esser (see note 95), pp. 146ff.; Stamm (see note 88), pp. 60ff.; van Straaten 1988 (see note 6), pp. 60-63 and 74f.; Friedman (see note 51), pp. 176ff.; Troy (see note 96), pp. 81ff.

107 Oud (see note 88), pp. 74ff.; Stamm (see note 88), pp. 69ff.

108 See Oud (see note 88), pp. 79ff.; Stamm (see note 88), pp. 76f.; Fanelli (see note 88), pp. 93ff.

109 Oud (see note 88), pp. 88ff.; Stamm (see note 88), pp. 80ff.; Fanelli (see note 88), pp. 98f.

110 Fanelli (see note 88), pp. 93ff. and 134-139, Oud (see note 88), pp. 78f.; Stamm (see note 88), pp. 74ff.

111 Fanelli (see note 88), pp. 93ff. and 170-173; Oud (see note 88), pp. 84ff.; Stamm (see note 88), pp. 77ff. Since then the café was rebuilt with its original façade at No. 25, Mauritsweg.

112 The Oud archives of the Nederlands Documentatiecentrum voor de Bouwkunst in Amsterdam contain two drafts for the façade under the inventory number 38 III. These show that Oud had originally planned the large red plane without subdivisions. A further draft is shown in Friedman (see note 51), illus. 19 (with the line grid).

113 Friedman (see note 51), pp. 182f.; *De Nieuwe Beelding* catalogue (see note 89), pp. 57f.; Troy (see note 96), pp. 91ff.; van Straaten 1988 (see note 6), pp. 76ff.; van Straaten 1983 (see note 6), pp. 102ff.; Allan Doig, *Theo van Doesburg. Painting into Architecture, Theory into Practice*, Cambridge 1986, pp. 82ff.

114 Hellen Zeeders and Jan Cees Nauta, *Theo van Doesburg in Drachten*, Drachten 1988.

115 Fanelli (see note 88), pp. 70f.; Friedman (see note 51), pp. 184, 186f.; Troy (see note 96), pp. 98ff.; van Straaten 1988 (see note 6), pp. 146ff.; Doig (see note 113), pp. 141ff.

116 After Bart van der Leck, who left *De Stijl* as early as 1918, the group was left by Wils, van 't Hoff and Huszár in 1919. Huszár, however, sporadically joined the group again at a later stage. Fanelli (see note 88), p. 41.

117 Fanelli (see note 88), pp. 42ff.; Godoli (see note 101), pp. 50f.; Friedman (see note 51), p. 100; Sjarel Ex and Els Hoek in: Blotkamp (see note 6), pp. 198ff.

118 Fanelli (see note 88), pp. 37ff.; Esser in: Blotkamp (see note 6), pp. 138ff.; Oud (see note 88), pp. 47ff.; Stamm (see note 88), pp. 44ff.

119 Fanelli (see note 88), p. 27ff.; Troy (see note 96), pp. 34ff.; Ex/Hoek (see note 6), pp. 55ff.; Kees Broos, *Piet Zwart*, 2nd edition, Amsterdam 1982, pp. 14ff.; Friedman (see note 51), p. 172.

120 *De Stijl* 5, No. 5, 1922, p. 78.

121 Zwart criticized the *De Stijl* movement in an article in *Elsevier's Geillustreerde Maandschrift*. Van Doesburg replied in *De Stijl* 2, No. 12, 1919, p. 144 by describing Zwart contemptuously as a reactionary and "supporter of the Viennese style". It is indeed true that Zwart was influenced by the furniture design of the Viennese Secessionists, and this can be seen in the armchairs of the sitting room in *De Arends-*

hoeve of 1921 (cf. note 124). Van Doesburg's remark certainly proves that he knew the art of the Viennese Secessionists very well indeed! (Cf. also note 39 on this subject.)

122 Sjarel Ex in: Blotkamp (see note 6), pp. 102-104.

123 Ex in: Blotkamp (see note 6), pp. 104ff.; Ex/Hoek (see note 6), p. 56ff., Troy (see note 96), pp. 36ff.

124 Ex in: Blotkamp (see note 6), pp. 106f.; Ex/Hoek (see note 6), pp. 55ff., illus. 91 and 92; Broos (see note 119), p. 20. The leather armchairs were copied by Zwart from the ones designed by Josef Hoffmann in 1905 for the Great Hall at the *Palais Stoclet* in Brussels. Varnedoe (see note 39), p. 67.

125 The same chair also figured in a design for a women's residence (1920), though this project was never executed. Troy (see note 96), p. 53; Friedman (see note 51), p. 172; Broos (see note 119), p. 18; Fanelli (see note 88), p. 44.

126 Theodore M. Brown, *The Work of G. Rietveld Architect*, Utrecht 1958, p. 13; Marijke Küper in: Blotkamp (see note 6), pp. 260f.; Marijke Küper (ed.), *Rietveld als meubelmaker, wonen met experimenten, 1900–1924*, exhibition catalogue, Utrecht 1983, p. 2.

127 Brown (see note 126), p. 16; Daniele Baroni, I mobili di Gerrit Thomas Rietveld, Milan 1977, p. 33 (with the false statement that Rietveld also designed the furniture he had built for Klaarhamer); Küper in: Blotkamp (see note 6), pp. 262f.

128 Cf. the most detailed historical analysis of the genesis and the forms of the *Red/Blue Chair* in Jutter Wohlers, *Gerrit Rietveld als Möbelentwerfer,* M.A. thesis, University of Göttingen 1990 (typed manuscript), pp. 58ff.; also Küper in: Blotkamp (see note 6), pp. 263ff.; discussions in Fanelli (see note 88), pp. 123–128 and especially Baroni (see note 127), pp. 33ff. are very faulty. Our presentation follows the corrections by Wohlers (whom I would like to thank for pointing this out).

129 *De Stijl* 2, No. 11, 1919, *Bijlage XXII* (with an analysis by Theo van Doesburg).

130 See note 129.

131 Baroni (see note 127), pp. 30ff.; Küper in: Blotkamp (see note 6), pp. 272ff.; Wohlers (see note 128), pp. 88ff.; Friedman (see note 51), p. 132. Together with the prototype of the *Red/Blue Chair*, this *Sideboard* formed part of a model flat in Spangen. Cf. note 105.

132 Friedman (see note 51), p. 134; Baroni (see note 127), p. 62; Brown (see note 126), pp. 82-84; Wohlers (see note 128), pp. 84ff.

133 Friedman (see note 51), p. 134; Küper in: Blotkamp (see note 6), p. 282; Baroni (see note 127), pp. 159f.; Wohlers (see note 128), pp. 51ff.

134 Friedman (see note 51), p. 134; Baroni (see note 127), p. 92; Wohlers (see note 128), pp. 54ff.

135 Van Straaten 1988 (see note 6), pp. 66ff.; Küpper in: Blotkamp (see note 6), p. 267; Troy (see note 96), pp. 43f.; van Straaten 1983 (see note 6), pp. 90f.; Doig (see note 113), pp. 147f.

136 Friedman (see note 51), pp. 107 and 133; Brown (see note 126), p. 24; Baroni (see note 127), p. 45; Küper in: Blotkamp (see note 6), pp. 271f.; Wohlers (see note 128); pp. 46f.; Fanelli (see note 88), p. 40. See also note 166 on the light.
The interior design of this room immediately became known internationally. It was also mentioned by Bruno Taut in his book *Die Neue Wohnung. Die Frau als Schöpferin* (The New Home. The Woman as Creator), Leipzig 1924, p. 37. In this book he particularly discusses the spatial effect of the large sphere on the wall.

137 Troy (see note 96), p. 166; Ex/Hoek (see note 6), pp. 68ff.; Ex in: Blotkamp (see note 6), pp. 107ff.

138 Fanelli (see note 88), pp. 130ff.; Troy (see note 96), p. 53.

139 Brown (see note 126), pp. 76f., illus. 82.

140 Ex/Hoek (see note 6), illus. 134; Ex in: Blotkamp (see note 6), p. 116.

141 Ex/Hoek (see note 6), pp. 131ff.

142 Friedman (see note 51), pp. 136ff.; Fanelli (see note 88), pp. 86ff. and 157-169; Bertus Mulder/Gerrit Jan de Rook/Carel Blotkamp, *Rietveld-Schröderhuis 1925–1975*, Utrecht/Antwerp 1975; *rietveld architect*, exhibition catalogue, Amsterdam 1971, no. 36; Paul Overy/Lenneke Büller/Frank den Oudsten/Bertus Mulder, *The Rietveld Schröder House*, Braunschweig 1988; Brown (see note 126), Wohlers (s. n. 128), pp. 77ff.; *Rietveld Schröder Archief*, exhibition catalogue, Utrecht 1988, pp. 13ff.

143 For a general survey cf. Corrie Nagtegaal, *Tr. Schröder-Schräder, Bewoonster van het Rietveld Schröderhuis*, Utrecht 1987.

144 Our discussion follows Fanelli (see note 88), Mulder et al. (see note 142) and Overy et al. (see note 142).

145 Brown (see note 126), p. 79; *Rietveld Schröder Archief* (see note 142), pp. 149ff. The interior is now lost, except for the bedroom which has been in the Stedelijk Museum, Amsterdam, since 1971.

146 Fanelli (see note 88), pp. 86ff.; Brown (see note 126), *rietveld architect* (see note 142), no. 47.

147 Fanelli (see note 88), pp. 86ff.; Brown (see note 126), pp. 86-89, Fritz Bless, *Rietveld 1888–1964. Een biografie*, Amsterdam 1982, p. 85; *rietveld architect* (see note 142), no. 62.

148 Fanelli (see note 88), pp. 86ff.; Brown (see note 126), pp. 93-98; *rietveld architect* (see note 142), no. 68.

149 Wim de Wit, *Expressionismus in Holland. Die Architektur der Amsterdamer Schule*, Stuttgart 1986; J.J. Vriend, *Amsterdamer Schule*, Amsterdam 1970.

150 Friedman (see note 51), p. 173; Troy (see note 96), pp. 53ff.; Broos (see note 119), p. 22; Fanelli (see note 88), p. 44.

151 Fanelli (see note 88), p. 40; Brown (see note 126), pp. 24f.; Küper in: Blotkamp (see note 6), pp. 269f.

152 Friedman (see note 51), p. 160; Ex/Hoek (see note 6), p. 118.

153 Ex/Hoek (see note 6), pp. 113ff.

154 Quoted from the foundation manifesto for the "Constructivist International Creative Co-opeative" in *De Stijl* 5, No. 8, 1922, p. 114.

155 *De Stijl* 1, No. 2, 1917, pp. 18ff.; 1, No. 4 (recte: no. 3), 1918, pp. 27ff.; 1, No. 4, 1918, pp. 45ff.; 1, No. 5, 1918, pp. 59ff.; 1, Nr. 8, 1918, pp. 94ff.

156 *De Stijl* 1, No. 2, 1917, p. 19; Oud's article on "Art and Machine" in issue 3, pp. 25ff.

157 According to research into the history of publishing, *De Stijl* had a circulation of about 400 copies around 1922 and reached its maximum in 1927, with about 700 copies. However, this was quite a lot for an avant-garde artists' journal. Also, the readership consisted mainly of people who were professionally involved in art themselves, so that the ideas of *De Stijl* were guaranteed to spread. See also Michael Schumacher, "Avantgarde und Öffentlichkeit. Zur Soziologie der Künstlerzeitschrift am Beispiel von *De Stijl*", doctoral thesis, Aachen 1979, pp. 214ff.

158 I.K. Bonset already introduced his new poetry in issue 1, 1921, pp. 1ff. His poetry consisted mainly of the sound images of letters. His contributions continued to be published in serialized form throughout that year. Aldo Camini published his *Caminoscopie*, also in a series, from issue 5, 1921, pp. 65ff. onwards. "Zelfmoord en Kleptomanie" (Suicide and Kleptomania) by I.K. Bonset was published in issue 4, 1921, p. 50; and Theo van Doesburg discussed abstract films by Hans Richter and Viking Eggeling in issue 5, 1921, p. 71.

159 For a general survey, cf. Fanelli (see note 88), pp. 60ff.; also Baljeu (see note 31), pp. 39ff.; van Straaten 1983 (see note 6), pp. 98ff.; Jaffé (see note 4), pp. 194ff.

160 Van Doesburg explained his views on the *Bauhaus* and the history of *De Stijl*'s influence in a long article on the development of the movement's influence abroad. This article appeared in the anniversary issue 79–84, 1927, pp. 53ff., especially pp. 53-55; cf. also Fanelli (see note 88), pp. 60ff.

161 Cf. also van Straaten 1983 (see note 6), p. 101.

162 Cf. Fanelli (see note 88), p. 61.

163 Fanelli (see note 88), pp. 61ff. (a letter from

Feininger); van Straaten 1983 (see note 6), pp. 103f.; van Straaten 1988 (see note 6), pp. 102ff.; Baljeu (see note 31), pp. 41ff.

164 Fanelli (see note 88), p. 63; van Straaten 1988 (see note 6), Nos. XXII and XXIII.

165 For a general survey of the history and structure of *Bauhaus* cf. Magdalena Droste, *Das Bauhaus, 1919–1933*, Cologne 1990; Hans M. Wingler, *Das Bauhaus 1919–1933. Weimar Dessau Berlin und die Nachfolge in Chicago seit 1937*, 2nd edition, Bramsche/Cologne 1968.

166 Sembach/Leuthäuser/Gössel (see note 39), pp. 94ff.

167 Piet Mondrian, *Neue Gestaltung*, Munich 1925 (= *Bauhausbücher*, volume 5), new edition, ed. by H.M. Wingler, Mainz 1974 (=*Neue Bauhausbücher*); Theo van Doesburg, *Grundbegriffe der neuen gestaltenden Kunst*, Munich 1925 (=*Bauhausbücher*, volume 6), new edition, ed. by H.M. Wingler, Mainz 1966 (=*Neue Bauhausbücher*); J.J.P. Oud, *Holländische Architektur*, Munich 1926 (=*Bauhausbücher*, volume 10), new edition, ed. by H.M. Wingler, Mainz 1976 (=*Neue Bauhausbücher*).

168 Fanelli (see note 88), pp. 64f.; van Straaten 1983 (see note 6), pp. 104-111; Baljeu (see note 31), pp. 49ff.

169 *De Stijl* 5, No. 8, 1922, pp. 113-128.

170 Fanelli (see note 88), pp. 64f.; Baljeu (see note 31), pp. 53-55.

171 Baljeu (see note 31), pp. 55ff.; Doig (see note 113), pp. 125 and 134ff.; Friedman (see note 51), pp. 146ff.; *El Lissitzky 1890–1941, Retrospective*, exhibition catalogue, Frankfurt/Main 1988, pp. 44ff.

172 *El Lissitzky Retrospective* (see note 171), pp. 190ff.; Troy (see note 96), pp. 124ff.

173 Sophie Lissitzky-Küppers, *El Lissitzky*, Dresden 1967, p. 361; *El Lissitzy Retrospective* (see note 171), p. 190.

174 Friedman (see note 51), p. 173; Fanelli (see note 88), p. 76; Troy (see note 96), pp. 129ff.; Ex/Hoek (see note 6), pp. 75ff.

175 Fanelli (see note 88), pp. 70ff.; Friedman (see note 51), pp. 90f.; Troy (see note 96), pp. 114ff.; Baljeu (see note 31), pp. 58ff.; van Straaten 1983 (see note 6), pp. 118ff.

176 Fanelli (see note 88), pp. 72f.

177 For a general survey cf. Fanelli (see note 88), pp. 71f.; Doig (see note 113), pp. 149ff.

178 Fanelli (see note 88), pp. 140ff.; van Straaten 1988 (see note 6), pp. 108ff.; Troy (see note 96), pp. 106ff.

179 Fanelli (see note 88), pp. 142f.; van Straaten (see note 6), pp. 114ff.; Troy (see note 96), pp. 108ff.

180 Fanelli (see note 88), pp. 143ff.; van Straaten 1988 (see note 6), pp. 138ff.; Troy (see note 96), pp. 114f.

181 Fanelli (see note 88), p. 155.

182 For exact references cf. Fanelli (see note 88), pp. 146, 149 and 150.

183 Troy (see note 96), p. 110.

184 Fanelli (see note 88), p. 143; Troy (see note 96), p. 110; van Straaten (see note 6), pp. 114ff.

185 Stanislaus von Moos, *Le Corbusier. Elemente einer Synthese*, Frauenfeld/Stuttgart 1968, pp. 49ff.; William J.R. Curtis, *Le Corbusier, Ideas and Forms*, New York 1986, pp. 42ff.; on the responses to the *De Stijl* exhibition in general cf. Fanelli (see note 88), pp. 75f.; *Het Nieuwe Bouwen* (see note 89), pp. 101ff.

186 Von Moos (see note 185), pp. 90ff.; Curtis (see note 185), pp. 60ff.

187 Fanelli (see note 88), p. 76.

188 Yve-Alain Bois in: *Het Nieuwe Bouwen* (see note 89), p. 104.

189 D. Deshoulières and H. Janneau (eds.), *Robert Mallet-Stevens – Architecte*, Brussels 1980.

190 Bois (see note 188), pp. 111f.

191 Friedmann (see note 51), pp. 172f.; van Straaten 1988 (see note 6), pp. 176ff.; Doig (see note 113), pp. 168ff.

192 Bois (see note 188), pp. 112f.

193 Bois (see note 188), p. 113.

194 Fanelli (see note 88), pp. 75f. and 79; Baljeu (see note 31), p. 71.

195 Fanelli (see note 88), pp. 95ff.

196 Troy (see note 96), pp. 135ff.; H. Henkels in: Mondrian Catalogue 1980 (see note 71), pp. 259ff.

197 Troy (see note 96), p. 142; Friedman (see note 51), p. 180.

198 Troy (see note 96), pp. 142ff.; Friedman (see note 51), pp. 180ff.

199 Troy (see note 96), pp. 161ff.

200 Troy (see note 96), p. 164.

201 Cf. note 83 and Hans L.C. Jaffé, *Vordemberge-Gildewart. Mensch und Werk*, Cologne 1971, especially p. 23.

202 Werner Graeff first published in *De Stijl* 6, Nos. 3/4, 1923, pp. 41ff.; Hans Richter in 4, No. 7, 1921, pp. 109ff.; Karl Peter Röhl in 4, No. 9, 1921, pp. 143f.; cf. also *Mondrian and De Stijl* (see note 66), pp. 38ff., 86ff., 241 and 247f.

203 Fawcett (see note 46), pp. 33-44; Schumacher (see note 157), pp. 203–206.

204 Quoted by Fanelli (see note 88), p. 102.

205 Fanelli (see note 88), pp. 99ff.; Baljeu (see note 31), pp. 53ff.

206 Fanelli (see note 88), pp. 103ff.; Friedman (see note 51), pp. 190ff.; Baljeu (see note 31), pp. 83ff.; Troy (see note 96), pp. 168ff.; van Straaten 1983 (see note 6), pp. 145ff.; van Straaten 1988 (see note 6), pp. 196ff.

207 Fanelli (see note 88), pp. 174-180; Pierre Georgel and Edmée de Lillers, *Theo van Doesburg: Projets pour l'Aubette*, Paris 1977.

208 Quoted from Fanelli (see note 88), p. 104.

209 Jürgen Joedicke und Christian Plath, *Die Weißenhofsiedlung*, Stuttgart 1977.

210 Oud (see note 88), pp. 98ff.; Stamm (see note 88), pp. 85ff.

211 Friedman (see note 51), p. 92; Baljeu (see note 31), pp. 88ff.; van Straaten 1983 (see note 6), pp. 170ff.; van Straaten 1988 (see note 6), pp. 236ff.; Doig (see note 113), pp. 199ff.

Literature

Baljeu, Joost, *Theo van Doesburg*, London/New York 1974

Banham, Reyner, *Die Revolution der Architektur. Theorie und Gestaltung im ersten Maschinenzeitalter*, Reinbek 1964

Baroni, Daniele, *I mobili di Gerrit Thomas Rietveld*, Milan 1977

Bless, Fritz, *Rietveld 1888–1964. Een biografie*, Amsterdam 1982

Blijstra, R., *C. van Eesteren*, Amsterdam 1971

Blok, Cornelis, *Piet Mondrian: Een catalogus van zijn werk in Nederlands openbaar bezit*, Amsterdam 1974

Blotkamp, Carel (ed.), *De Stijl: 1917–1922. The Formative Years*, Cambridge/Mass. and London 1986

Blotkamp, Carel, *Mondrain in Detail*, Utrecht/Antwerp 1987

Bool, Flip and Kees Broos, *Domela: Paintings, Reliefs, Sculptures, Graphic Work, Typography, Photographs*, The Hague 1980

Broos, Kees, *Piet Zwart 1885–1977*, 2nd edition, Amsterdam 1982

Brown, Theodore, *The Work of Gerrit Rietveld, Architect*, Utrecht 1958

Bulhof, F. (ed.), *De Stijl. Modernism in the Netherlands and Belgium in the First Quarter of the 20th Century*, The Hague 1976

Calvesi, Maurizio, *Futurismus*, Cologne 1987

Carmean, E.A. Jr., *Mondrian. The Diamond Compositions*, Washington 1979

Curtis, William J.R., *Le Corbusier. Ideas and Forms*, New York 1986

Daix, Pierre, *Der Kubismus in Wort und Bild*, Stuttgart 1982

Deshoulières, D., and H. Janneau (eds.), *Robert Mallet-Stevens - Architecte*, Brussels 1980

Deventer, S. van, *Kröller-Müller. De geschiedenis van een cultureel levenswerk*, Haarlem 1956

Dittmann, Lorenz, *Farbgestaltung und Farbtheorie in der abendländischen Malerei*, Darmstadt 1987

Theo van Doesburg 1883–1931, exhibition catalogue, Eindhoven 1968

Doesburg, Theo van, *Grundbegriffe der neuen gestaltenden Kunst*, Mainz/Berlin 1966

Doig, Allen, *Theo van Doesburg. Painting into Architecture, Theory into Practice*, Cambridge 1986

Droste, Magdalena, *Das Bauhaus 1917–1933*, Cologne 1990

Elgar, Frank, *Mondrian*, London 1968

Ex, Sjarel and Els Hoek, *Vilmos Huszár, schilder en ontwerper 1884–1960*, Utrecht 1985

Fanelli, Giovanni, *Moderne architectuur in Nederland 1900–1940*, 2nd edition, 's-Gravenhage 1981

Fanelli, Giovanni, *Stijl-Architektur. Der niederländische Beitrag zur frühen Moderne*, Stuttgart 1985

Fawcett, Trevor and Clive Phillpot (eds.), *The Art Press: Two Centuries of Art Magazines*, London 1976

Feltkamp, W.C., *B.A. van der Leck, leven en werken*, Leiden 1956

Fliedl, Gottfried, *Gustav Klimt*, English edition, Cologne 1990

Friedman, Mildred (ed.), *De Stijl 1917-1931. Visions of Utopia*, 2nd edition, Oxford 1986

Georgel, Pierre and Edmée de Lillers, *Theo van Doesburg: Projets pour l'Aubette*, Paris 1977

Giedion, Sigfried, *Die Herrschaft der Mechanisierung* (edited by H. Ritter), Frankfurt/M. 1987

Godoli, Ezio, *Jan Wils, Frank Lloyd Wright e De Stijl*, Calenzano 1980

Gombrich, Ernst Hans, *Aby Warburg. An Intellectual Biography*, London 1970

Graf, Otto Antonia, *Die Kunst des Quadrats. Zum Werk von Frank Lloyd Wright*, 2 volumes, Vienna 1983

Hedrick, Hannah, *Theo van Doesburg, Propagandist and Practitioner of the Avant-Garde, 1909–1923*, Ann Arbor 1980

Heinz, Rudolf, *Stil als geisteswissenschaftliche Kategorie. Problemgeschichtliche Untersuchungen zum Stilbegriff im 19. und 20. Jahrhundert*, Würzburg 1986

Hess, Walter, *Das Problem der Farbe in den Selbstzeugnissen der Maler von Cézanne bis Mondrian*, Mittenwald 1981

Hitchcock, Henry Russell and Philip Johnson, *The International Style, Architecture since 1922*, New York 1966

Robert van 't Hoff, exhibition catalogue, Eindhoven 1967 (leaflet)

Horst, Wouter van der, *Drachten heeft veel meer Stijl*, Drachten 1983

Hulten, Pontus (ed.), *Futurismo & Futurismi*, exhibition catalogue, Venice/Milan 1986

Jaffé, H.L.C., *De Stijl 1917–1931. Der niederländische Beitrag zur modernen Kunst*, Frankfurt/Main and Berlin 1965

Jaffé, H.L.C., *Mondrian und De Stijl*, Cologne 1967

Jaffé, H.L.C., *Vordemberge-Gildewart. Mensch und Werk*, Cologne 1971

Joedicke, Jürgen and Christian Plath, *Die Weißenhofsiedlung*, Stuttgart 1977

Küper, Marijke (ed.), *Rietveld als meubelmaker, wonen met experimenten 1900–1924*, exhibition catalogue, Utrecht 1983

Kunstenaren der idee – Symbolistische tendensen in Nederland, ca. 1880–1930, exhibition catalogue, 's-Gravenhage 1978

Lankheit, Klaus, *Das Triptychon als Pathosformel*, Heidelberg 1959

Bart van der Leck, 1876–1958, exhibition catalogue, Otterlo/Amsterdam 1976

Bart van der Leck, A la recherche de l'image des temps, exhibition catalogue, Institut Néerlandais, Paris 1980

El Lissitzky 1890–1941, Retrospektive, exhibition catalogue, Frankfurt/Main and Berlin 1988

Lissitzky-Küppers, Sophie, *El Lissitzky, Maler, Architekt, Typograf, Fotograf*, Dresden 1967

Mansbach, Steven A., *Visions of Totality, László Moholy-Nagy, Theo van Doesburg and El Lissitzky*, Ann Arbor 1980

Mondrian, Piet, *Plastic Art and Pure Plastic Art 1937 and Other Essays, 1941–1943*, 3rd edition, New York 1951

Mondrian, Piet, *Neue Gestaltung, Neoplastizismus, Nieuwe Beelding*, Mainz/Berlin 1974

Piet Mondrian Centennial Exhibition, exhibition catalogue, New York 1971

Mondrian and De Stijl, exhibition catalogue, Gmurzynska Gallery, Cologne 1979

Mondrian, Zeichnungen, Aquarelle, New Yorker Bilder, exhibition catalogue, Stuttgart 1980

Moos, Stanislaus von, *Le Corbusier. Elemente einer Synthese*, Frauenfeld/Stuttgart 1968

Mulder, Bertus, Gerrit Jan de Rook and Carel Blotkamp, *Rietveld Schröderhuis 1925–1975*, Antwerp 1975

Nagtegaal, Corrie, *Tr. Schröder-Schräder, bewoonster van het Rietveld Schröderhuis*, Utrecht 1987

Osterwold, Tilman, *Pop Art*, Cologne 1989

Ottolenghi, Maria Grazia, *Piet Mondrian, l'opera complete*, Milan 1974

Oud, Hans, *J.J.P. Oud. Architect 1890–1963*, 's-Gravenhage 1984

Oud, J.J.P., *Holländische Architektur*, Mainz/Berlin 1976

Overy, Paul, *De Stijl*, London/New York 1969

Overy, Paul, Lenneke Büller, Frank den Oudsten, Bertus Mulder, *The Rietveld Schröder House*, Braunschweig 1988

Oxenaar, R.W.D, "Bart van der Leck tot 1920. Een primitef van de nieuwe tijd", doctoral thesis, Utrecht 1976

Polano, Sergio (ed.), *Theo van Doesburg, Scritti di arte e di architettura*, Rome 1979

Purucker, G. von, *Theosophisches Wörterbuch*, Stuttgart 1949

Riedel, Ingrid, *Farben in Religion, Gesellschaft, Kunst und Psychotherapie*, Stuttgart/Berlin 1983

rietveld architect, exhibition catalogue, Amsterdam 1971

Rietveld Schröder Archief, exhibition catalogue, Utrecht 1988

Rot Gelb Blau. Die Primärfarben in der Kunst des 20. Jahrhunderts, exhibition catalogue, Kassel 1988

Rotzler, Willy, *Konstruktive Konzepte. Eine Geschichte der konstruktiven Kunst von Kubismus bis heute*, 2nd edition, Zurich 1988

Schippers, K., *Holland Dada*, Amsterdam 1974

Schumacher, Michael, "Avantgarde und Öffentlichkeit. Zur Soziologie der Künstlerzeitschrift am Beispiel von *De Stijl*", doctoral thesis, Aachen 1979

Sembach, Klaus-Jürgen, Gabriele Leuthäuser and Peter Gössel, *Möbeldesign des 20. Jahrhunderts*, Cologne 1988 *Twentieth-Century Furniture Design*, English edition, Cologne 1989

Gottfried Semper und die Mitte des 19. Jahrhunderts, Basle/Stuttgart 1976

Seuphor, Michel, *Piet Mondrian. Leben und Werk*, Cologne 1957

Stamm, Günther, *J.J.P. Oud, Bauten und Projekte 1906 bis 1963*, Mainz/Berlin 1984

De Stijl, 1917–1931, complete reprint in 2 volumes, 's-Gravenhage/Amsterdam 1968

De Nieuwe Beelding in de architectuur. Neoplasticism in Architecture. De Stijl, Delft 1983

Straaten, Evert van, *Theo van Doesburg 1883–1931*, 's-Gravenhage 1983

Straaten, Evert van, *Theo van Doesburg. Schilder en Architect*, 's-Gravenhage 1988.

thomas, angela, *denkbilder, materialien zur entwicklung von georges vantongerloo*, Düsseldorf 1987

Troy, Nancy J., *The De Stijl Environment*, Cambridge/Mass. and London 1983

Tuchman, Maurice and Judi Freeman (eds.), *Das Geistige in der Kunst. Abstrakte Malerei 1890-1985*, Stuttgart, 1988

Georges Vantongerloo. A Traveling Retrospective Exhibition, Brussels 1980

Varnedoe, Kirk, *Wien 1900, Kunst, Architektur & Design*, Cologne 1987

Vriend, J.J., *Amsterdamer Schule*, Amsterdam 1970

Walther, Ingo F., and Rainer Metzger, *Vincent van Gogh*, 2 volumes, Cologne 1989

Welsh, Robert P., *Piet Mondrian's Early Career. The "Naturalistic" Periods*, New York/London 1977

Weyergraf, Clara, *Piet Mondrian und Theo van Doesburg. Deutung von Werk und Theorie*, Munich 1979

Wijsenbeek, L.J.F., *Piet Mondrian*, Recklinghausen 1968

Wingler, Hans, *Das Bauhaus. 1919–1933. Weimar Dessau Berlin und die Nachfolge in Chicago seit 1937*, 2nd edition, Bramsche/Cologne 1968

Wismer, Beat, *Mondrians ästhetische Utopie*, Baden 1985

Wit, Wim de, *Expressionismus in Holland. Die Architektur der Amsterdamer Schule*, Stuttgart 1986

Wohlers, Jutta, "Gerrit Rietveld als Möbelentwerfer", M.A. thesis, University of Göttingen 1989
(typed manuscript)

Zeeders, Hellen and Jan Cees Nauta, *Theo van Doesburg in Drachten*, Drachten 1988

Zervos, Christian, *Domela*, Amsterdam 1966

Theo van Doesburg with his artist friends in Hanover
This photograph was taken at Hans Nitzschke's studio in 1925. Nitzschke can be seen at the front. Top: Nelly and Theo van Doesburg, middle (from left to right): Kurt Schwitters, Käthe Steinitz and Friedrich Vordemberge-Gildewart. Doesburg was commissioned by Alexander Dorner, director of Art Collections in Hanover, to design a stained glass window for a small exhibition room at the Provinzialmuseum.

Biographies

We have only listed those artists who belonged to De Stijl *or who participated in* De Stijl *projects.*

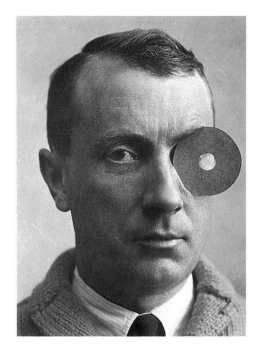

Jean (Hans) Arp

Cees Rinks de Boer

Born 16 September 1887 in Strasbourg. Studies at the Strasbourg School of Applied Arts. 1905 to 1907: studies under Ludwig von Hofmann, Weimar. 1908: Académie Julian, Paris. 1909: Moves to Switzerland where he founds an association called the *Moderner Bund* (first exhibition in Lucerne, 1911). 1912: associated with the *Blauer Reiter* in Munich, 1913: with Herwarth Walden's *Der Sturm* in Berlin. 1914: goes to Paris, where he meets Amedeo Modigliani, Max Jacob and Guillaume Apollinaire. Moves to Switzerland when war breaks out. 1915: first exhibition in Zurich, showing abstract and strictly geometrical works. 1916: co-founds *Dada* at the *Cabaret Voltaire*. 1921: marries Dadaist Sophie Taeuber. After First World War participates in several European *Dada* groups. 1925: takes part in the first Surrealists' exhibition in Paris, publishes several articles in art journals. Publishes book, *Die Kunst-Ismen* together with El Lissitzky. 1926–28: works on the design of *Café Aubette*, Strasbourg, together with his wife, Sophie Taueber-Arp, and Theo van Doesburg. From 1926: lives in Meudon. From 1931: three-dimensional sculptures; member of *Abstraction-Création*. 1940: flees from German troops to Grasse in southern France. 1942: Sophie Taeuber becomes ill. 1946: returns to Meudon, 1949–50: trip to U.S.A., 1952 and 1955: trips to Greece. 1950 and 1955: monumental reliefs for Harvard and Caracas Universities, wall relief for UNESCO in Paris. 1966: dies in Switzerland.

Born 3 August 1881 in Amsterdam. Goes to school in Drachten. Studies under H.H. Kramer. 1910: qualifies as architect and designs various buildings in Drachten (Kijlstraa bakery, Pruiksma barber's). From 1921: works on a number of middle-class houses and the Winter Agricultural School in Drachten. Restores churches in Drachten. 1929–40: also outside commissions (e.g. at Apeldoorn). Influenced originally by Art Nouveau, de Boer later carefully adapts to modern trends. Contacts with the Dadaist movement in the Netherlands, where he meets the Rinsema brothers and, through them, van Doesburg. 1966: dies on 4 January in Drachten.

Theo van Doesburg

Born 30 August 1883 as Emil Marie Küpper in Utrecht. Chooses pseudonym after his stepfather Theodorus Doesburg. Brief period at Cateau Esser's School of Dramatic Arts in Amsterdam, studying drama. From 1902: intends to be a freelance artist and writer. From 1912: publishes art reviews. Teaches himself art. Earliest paintings from 1904. 1914–16: national service on the Belgian border and in Utrecht, where he meets the writer and poet Anthony Kok and the philosopher Evert Rinsema. From early 1916: contacts with Oud, van der Leck, Huszár and Mondrian. Co-founds the De Sphinx group of artists. Collaborates on the house for Burgomaster de Broek in Waterland. 1917: moves to Leiden. 31 May 1917: second marriage, to Helena Milius, who works for a publishing company. Founds the art magazine De Stijl together with Leck, Huszár, Kok, Oud and Wils. Also works on several artistic projects with Oud (1917: Villa Allegonda in Katwijk aan Zee and De Vonk holiday residence in Noordwijkerhout, 1919–21: Spangen housing estate in Rotterdam), with Jan Wils (1917: Lange House in Alkmaar, a house in St. Antonius Polder, 1917–18: Leeuwaarden competition, 1918: De Dubbele Sleutel hotel/restaurant), with Rietveld (1919: Spangen housing estate, model flat, 1919: interior design for the De Eigt house in Katwijk aan Zee), with de Boer (middle-classs houses and agricultural college in Drachten). Editor-in-chief of De Stijl magazine from the first issue (October 1917, editorial office in Leiden, printed in Delft). Important De Stijl paintings. From 1920: articles on De Stijl under the pseudonym J.K. Bonset and from 1921 under the pseudonym Aldo Camini. From 1920: numerous propaganda trips to promote De Stijl's ideas in Belgium, France, Italy and Germany. Publishes Dadaist poems. March

1921: third marriage, to Nelly van Moorsel. End of 1921 in Berlin: contact with Bauhaus artists. 1922: tries in vain to become a lecturer at the Bauhaus and gives a De Stijl course in Weimar instead. Takes part in a Constructivist conference in Weimar in the same year. Links with El Lissitzky. Founds the Mécano magazine. 1923: moves to Paris and contributes to Mies van der Rohe's G magazine. Exhibition at the Rosenberg Gallery in Paris (together with van Eesteren, Huszár, Oud, Rietveld, van Leusden and Mies van der Rohe). Projects for three residential and studio houses. 1924: publishes architectural De Stijl manifesto in De Stijl. 1925: break with Mondrian. 1924: first solo exhibition of his paintings in Weimar; develops Elementarism. 1926: manifesto on Elementarism. 1926-28: collaboration with Jean Arp and Sophie Taeuber-Arp for the Café Aubette. 1929: founds the magazine L'Art Concret. 1929–30: builds residential and studio house in Meudon, designed according to his own plans. 1931: co-founds artists' group Abstraction-Création in Paris. 7 March 1931: dies in Paris, after a heart attack in Davos.

César Domela

Born 15 January 1900 in Amsterdam. 1919–20: earliest paintings, still in a Naturalist style. Self-taught artist. Spends 1922–23 in Switzerland; first abstract paintings. 1923: exhibits abstract works with the so-called November Group in Berlin. 1924: De Stijl member, after contacts with Mondrian and van Doesburg in Paris. 1927–33: lives and works in Berlin, though his works during this period, especially his wooden reliefs, are based on more complex principles of form than postulated by De Stijl. 1931: member of the group Abstraction-Création. From 1933: back in Paris, where he produces mainly Constructivist, polychrome reliefs. 1937: co-founds the magazine Plastiques together with Jean Arp and Sophie Taeuber. Exhibits at the first Salon des Réalités Nouvelles. 1946: founds the group Centre de Recherche (contacts with Poliakov, Schneider and Hartung). 1954: solo exhibition in Rio de Janeiro. 1955–60: wall reliefs at Utrecht insurance company's office in Rotterdam, designed by Oud. 1960: relief at De Nederlanden van 1845 insurance company's office in The Hague. Lives and works in Paris.

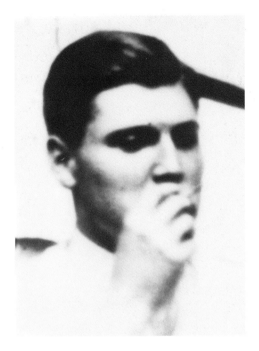

Cornelis van Eesteren

Born 4 July 1897 in Kinderdijk. Around 1915: works as a draughtsman at Willem Kromhout's studio in Rotterdam. 1917: graduates from the Academy of Fine Arts and Technical Sciences in Rotterdam. Works on municipal building projects in Alblasserdam. 1919: attends advanced course in Architecture V & HBO in Amsterdam. 1919–21: works for the architects W. Verschoor in The Hague and G.J. Rutgers in Amsterdam. 1921: Sponsorship Award for Fine Architecture. Uses the award to travel around Germany and Scandinavia. 1922: meets van Doesburg in Weimar. 1923: he is refused further scholarship payments. Works on projects for residential and studio houses together with van Doesburg. Takes part in *De Stijl* exhibition at Rosenberg Gallery in Paris. 1923–24: designs a house on a river and a house in Zorgvliet Park, The Hague; builds a one-family house in Kinderdijk. Attends course in *Hautes Etudes Urbaines* at the Sorbonne, Paris. 1924: tenders two projects for a shopping arcade in The Hague and the renovation of the *Rokin* in Amsterdam (together with Theo van Doesburg). 1925: wins award in competition for the redesigning of *Unter den Linden* in Berlin. 1924–27: office manager for architect Jan Wils. From 1925: also member of the Rotterdam group *Opbouw 2*. 1927–30: lecturer in town planning at the State School of Art in Weimar. 1927–29: contributions to the *i 10* magazine. From 1929 member of the Amsterdam group *De 8* and, from 1932, on the staff of the *De 8 en Opbouw* magazine. 1929–59: chief architect, town planner and head of the Amsterdam Town Planning Department. 1931–34: works on municipal building plans for Amsterdam, together with Th.K. van Lohuizen. These typical examples of rationalist town planning are approved in 1935. 1930–47: president of the International Congress of Mod-

ern Architecture (CIAM). 1949 and 1959–64: plans for the towns of Nagele and Lelystad. From 1947: professor at Delft Polytechnic. Dies on 21 February 1988.

Werner Graeff

Born 24 August 1901 in Wuppertal-Elberfeld, Germany. From 1921: at the Bauhaus in Weimar, where he primarily studies Industrial Design. 1922–30: member of *De Stijl*. Further studies at the College of Science and Technology in Berlin. Together with Hans Richter and Mies van der Rohe founder of *G*. Invents international road sign language, composes musical scores for abstract films, designs bodies for cars and motorcycles. 1925: member of the *Deutscher Werkbund* (German Factories Association). 1926–27: Chief of Press for *Die Wohnung* exhibition in Stuttgart; publishes there the books *Bau und Wohnung* and *Innenräume*. 1931–33: lecturer at the Reimann School in Berlin. 1934: moves to Spain, then to Switzerland. After the war, settles briefly in Paris. 1951–59: teaches at the Folkwang School in Essen, where his main field of work is with abstract murals. Dies on 29 August 1978 in Mülheim/Ruhr.

Robert van 't Hoff

Born 8 November 1887 in Rotterdam. Meets Frederik van Eeden's *Walden* housing association on a visit with his parents. 1904: meets the building contractor Pastunink, who then works together with him on his first building projects. 1906–11: studies at the School of Art, Birmingham. 1911–14: studies at the London Architectural Association; meets English avant-garde artists. First drafts of his own. 1913: his father gives him a copy of Frank Lloyd Wright's Wasmuth edition. June 1913 – July 1914: U.S.A., where he meets Frank Lloyd Wright. 1914–15: Huis ter Heide, where he builds the *Verloop* summer house. 1914–19: builds the so-called *Concrete House*, i.e. *Villa Henny*. 1916: first contacts with Theo van Doesburg and Oud. 1917: founding member of *De Stijl*. 1917–18: builds his own house boat, called *De Stijl*, with *De Stijl* interior design. 1918: designs a studio for Bart van der Leck. 1918–19: designs middle-class and council housing estates together with Klaarhamer. Autumn 1919: tries to gain support for Soviet artists in an international campaign together with P. Alma. Breaks with van Doesburg, due to the latter's negative attitude, leaves *De Stijl*, sells his house boat of the same name and builds two houses in the traditional style for himself and his parents in Laren. Designs simple furniture for these houses. 1922: moves to the U. K. 1928: unsuccessful attempt to set up a community in Cooperburg, Pennsylvania. Returns to Laren. 1931: moves to Switzerland and in 1937 finally to the U. K., where he designs plans for a housing association. 25 April 1979: dies in New Milton in the south of England.

Vilmos Huszár

Bart Anthony van der Leck

Pieter Jan Christophel Klaarhamer

Born 5 January 1884 in Budapest as Vilmos Herz, but calls himself Huszár from 1904. Studies to be a wall decorator at the Budapest School of Art. 1904: starts a course at the Munich Academy of Art. 1909: moves to the Netherlands where he lives and works in Voorburg until 1939 and then in Hierden, near Harderwijk, until his death. 1915–16: experiments with Cubist design principles. 1916: first drafts for stained glass windows. 1917: first abstract compositions. 1917: co-founder of *De Stijl*. Designs the logo for the magazine. 1918: first conflicts with van Doesburg, due to his colour design for the interior of van 't Hoff's *De Stijl* house boat. In opposition to Vantongerloo. 1918: first interior design for the industrialist Bruynzeel's house, together with Pieter Klaarhamer. Also designs exhibition stall for Bruynzeel's company in Utrecht. 1919–21: several drafts for interior designs, partly together with Jan Wils (Bersenbrugge photographic studio in The Hague), Piet Zwart (Bruynzeel's living room and a residential home for single mothers in The Hague) and van der Kloot Meyburg (house in Voorburg). Contributes some of these drafts to the *De Stijl* exhibition at the Rosenberg Gallery in Paris. 1921: joins Rietveld in participating in a subsidiary exhibition of the Greater Berlin Art Exhibition. As early as 1921: international contacts. Takes part in the Constructivists' meeting in Düsseldorf together with van Doesburg. Meets El Lissitzky. Trip to Paris. From c. 1925: graphic designs for advertising and industry, including a draft from the Miss Blanche cigarette campaign, and designs for exhibition posters. Also, from 1927, an increasing number of paintings, and from 1930 furniture designs for Metz & Co. Dies in 1960.

Born in Swiep in 1874. School of Applied Arts in Utrecht. Works in several different studios, including P.J.H. Cuypers' in Amsterdam. From 1902: freelance architect in Utrecht. 1905: graphic designs for a magazine, together with Bart van der Leck. Teaches evening classes at the Utrecht School of Applied Arts. Later, 1908–11, Rietveld is one of his students. From 1913: explores ways of using ferroconcrete in residential architecture. 1918–19: together with van 't Hoff takes part in residential building projects, using ferroconcrete. These houses are intended for middle-class and working-class residents. (First publication of one of his projects in 1926 in Oud's Bauhaus book.) 1918: together with Huszár, designs boys' bedroom for the industrialist Bruynzeel's house in Voorburg. From 1920s: residential housing estates in the Utrecht area. 1954: dies in Ede.

Born 26 November 1876 in Utrecht. Leaves school at the age of 14. 1891–99: works at glass painter's workshop, where he meets Piet Klaarhamer in 1893. 1900–04: Amsterdam School of Applied Arts and evening classes at the State Academy of Art. 1905: returns to Utrecht. Designs furniture and illustrations for a book edition of the *Song of Songs* together with Klaarhamer. 1907: spends two weeks in Paris, trying in vain to settle down there. 1908: works in Glanerburg on the German border. April 1909 – June 1915: Amersfoort, and from 1912 stylized forms and the use of colour planes. From 1914: various jobs for Kröller-Müller company, and as part of his activities, a trip to southern Spain and Algeria from April to June 1914. Designs stained glass windows for Kröller-Müller. 1916–17: differences of opinion with the architect Berlage while working on the interior design for the Kröller-Müller building. March 1916: completion of the painting *The Storm*. The painting, which belongs to Mrs Müller, is made accessible to the public in The Hague from April 1916 onwards. Lives and works in The Hague until April 1916, then moves to Laren where he stays until May 1919. Meets Mondrian, van Doesburg and the theosophist Dr. Schoenmaekers. Already knows Huszár and Chris Beekman from the *Haagsche Kunstkring* (Hague Artists' Circle) 1915–1917; founding member of *De Stijl*, contributions to the *De Stijl* magazine. 1918: refuses to sign the first *De Stijl* manifesto, breaks with van Doesburg and *De Stijl*. Lives in Blaricum, in a house and studio designed by himself, from May 1918 until his death. Paints abstractions of representational motifs again. From 1928: designs furniture and materials for Metz & Co. 1930s: experimental works in ceramics for Delft Salad Oil Manufacturers, together with the painter H.M. Kamerlingh. 1958: dies in Blaricum.

Willem van Leusden

El Lissitzky

Born in Utrecht in 1886. Studies painting at the academy in The Hague. 1911: member of the *Kunstliefde* (Love of Art) society in Utrecht, where he probably has contact with Rietveld. From 1915: Impressionist beginnings, then Cubist forms. 1920: geometrical/abstract compositions under the influence of van der Leck's work. Designs wall decoration for a dancing school. From c. 1922: works on architectural models. 1923: three of his models are shown at the *De Stijl* exhibition at the Rosenberg Gallery in Paris (designs for a transformer station, a garage with a kiosk and a public lavatory with a transformer station). Writes articles for *De Stijl* and *L'Architecture Vivante*. 1927: publishes four photos of a model for a little tea house in a municipal park, designed in 1924. From 1930: Surrealist paintings. Dies in Maarssen.

Born in Smolensk on 23 November 1890 (modern calendar) as Lazar Mordukhovich Lissitzky. Local grammar school in Smolensk. Tries in vain to gain access to the St. Petersburg Academy of Art. From 1909: course in architecture at the Darmstadt Technical College, Germany. Extensive trips through Germany, France and Italy. Returns to Russia at the outbreak of the First World War. 1914–18: course at Riga Polytechnic. 3 June 1918: diploma in architecture and engineering. Also works at an architectural studio while at university. 1916 – mid-1919: supports Jewish Renaissance (a movement for the revival of Jewish national culture). Paints and designs illustrations, among other things. 1917: takes part in the two revolutions. After the February Revolution becomes a member of the cultural department of the Moscow Soviet, and after the October Revolution the Fine Arts Department of *Narkompros*. 1919: moves to Kiev and accepts a professorship in graphic design, printing and architecture at the People's School of Art in Vitebsk, founded by Marc Chagall. Encounters Kazimir Malevich and his Suprematism. Under the influence of opponents of Chagall. Suprematist posters. 1921: head of the Faculty of Architecture at the Vkhutemas School of Art in Moscow. Meets van Doesburg in Berlin. From 1920: works on a children's book, *Of Two Squares*. 1922: takes part in the International Congress of Progressive Artists in Düsseldorf and the Constructivists's Congress in Weimar. Autumn 1922: takes part in the First Russian Art Exhibition in Berlin at the Van Diemen Gallery (shown in Amsterdam in spring 1923). Spring 1923: lectures on modern Russian art in the Netherlands (repeated in June of the same year). 1923: designs a *Proun Room* for the Greater Berlin Art Exhibition. Moves to Hanover and meets Sophie Küppers, whom he marries in

1927. Early 1923: first solo exhibition at the Kestner Society in Hanover. Makes friends with Dadaist Kurt Schwitters. Publishes in *De Stijl*. From 1923: photographic experiments. 1923–25: stays in Locarno, Switzerland, to recover from tuberculosis. 1925: returns to the Soviet Union. Architectural projects. 1926: designs exhibition rooms for the International Art Exhibition in Dresden. 1927–28: designs *Abstract Cabinet* for the State Gallery of Lower Saxony in Hanover (destroyed by the Nazis in 1937 and reconstructed recently). 1928: chief artist of the international printing exhibition *Pressa* in Cologne. From September 1929: architect, from 1930 chief architect, of the Central Park of Culture and Recreation in Moscow. Numerous architectural works, designs for propaganda campaigns and exhibitions. 21 December 1941: dies in Moscow.